Feng Shui

for Business & Office

Feng Shui

for Business & Office

Dr. Jes T.Y. Lim

Warwick Publishing

Feng Shui for Business & Office

We acknowledge the financial support of the Government of Canada through the Book Publishing Industry Development Program for our publishing activities.

ISBN: 1-894622-24-3

Published by Warwick Publishing Inc.
161 Frederick Street
Toronto, Ontario M5A 4P3 Canada
www.warwickgp.com

Distributed in the United States by:
Weatherhill, Inc.
41 Monroe Turnpike
Trumbull, CT 06611 USA

Distributed in Canada by:
Canadian Book Network
c/o Georgetown Terminal Warehouses
34 Armstrong Avenue
Georgetown, Ontario L7G 4R9 Canada

Design: Clint Rogerson
Illustrations: Luisa Klein, Munich, Germany; Robert F. Künzler, Munich, Germany
Printed and bound in Canada

CONTENTS

ACKNOWLEDGEMENTS

I would like to extend my gratitude to the owners, managers and chief executives of the many companies, large and small, who, over the last thirty years have put their trust in my Feng Shui knowledge. To maintain confidentiality, it is not possible for me to mention the names of these highly valued clients.

By allowing me to implement Feng Shui technologies and remedies in order to test their effectiveness, they have enabled me to adapt my knowledge to the business requirements for the challenging twenty-first century. The wisdom I have gained has been the foundation for the establishment of the QI-MAG International Feng Shui and Geobiology Institute, where I now share my knowledge with committed participants and students from around the world.

My thanks also go to all the readers for their support for my first book, *Feng Shui and Your Health*, published by Times Publishing, Singapore, and to Joy Verlag for the German edition in 1997.

Last but not least, my love and heartfelt thanks go to my wife, Julie, for her support in accompanying me for more than six months each year on my busy teaching schedule around the world.

And to the readers of this book, may I encourage you to share this knowledge as widely as possible in order to promote a "win-win" philosophy and so contribute to achieving world peace.

My wish for you is a healthy, long life full of fun, love, happiness and success.

Prof. Dr. Jes T.Y. Lim
Shanghai, China

Preface

During almost thirty years of working as a business consultant, I have found that more than eighty per cent of the problems of unprofitable companies are caused by Feng Shui imbalances. Specific Feng Shui measures have helped many companies to return to profitability. My study of companies that have gone bankrupt has shown similar results. Good knowledge of Business Feng Shui could therefore prevent up to eighty per cent of bankruptcies worldwide.

Since the 1980s, Feng Shui, the ancient Chinese science and art of healthy living and successful working, has been rediscovered by many people in Asia, as well as in Australia and Great Britain. But Feng Shui is not really anything new in North America and parts of Europe, because many old buildings there were built according to principles of geomancy that come close to the principles of Feng Shui.

However, outside traditional Chinese family circles the teachings of Business Feng Shui are less known. At the emperor's court of ancient China they were a well-kept secret. The Feng Shui knowledge of the officials and business people was exclusively passed on from masters to selected students or within a family clan. I was very lucky to learn from three old masters who were experts in this field.

In this book I will explain various aspects and guidelines of Business Feng Shui practice, including aspects that are seldom mentioned elsewhere. Thus you have the opportunity to avoid making mistakes, and to use remedies where necessary, if you or your staff are confronted with seemingly insurmountable problems. Even if you just have a vague feeling that your business is not running as smoothly as it could, Business Feng Shui will provide you with solid, practical steps you can take to make the energies flow again.

CHAPTER I
What is Business Feng Shui?

The basic term "Feng Shui" (pronounced *fung shway*) is derived from two Chinese characters Feng (wind) and Shui (water), and was coined by ancient Taoist masters living in the mountains of China who were researching the conditions for human longevity. They were studying the effects of wind, water and the environment on humans.

"Wind" covers the types and quality of air, space, light, astrology and planetary movements. "Water" includes mountain formations, water flow, rivers, lakes, and everything else that is of the earth.

For a long time Feng Shui was supported by the Chinese imperial government in order to study the effects of wind, weather and environmental conditions on humans, especially on soldiers in the battlefields.

Over the last 5,000 years Feng Shui has been developed into a most profound living and working science. Feng Shui is the accepted consciousness of many people and is practiced by 1.3 billion Chinese plus other Asians — for example, Japanese and Koreans — and also by Europeans. Feng Shui therefore is a reality and you will be affected by this consciousness whether you believe in it or not.

How Feng Shui supports you
Like everything we do in our life, when we are fully committed mentally, emotionally, physically and spiritually to a task, we certainly perform well and achieve faster

results. Feng Shui practice follows similar principles. The more you commit and put your effort into it, the faster and better it works. Even if you don't believe in the practice of Feng Shui, many natural phenomena and conditions in your environment and your belief systems still affect you.

In my first book, *Feng Shui and Your Health*, I explained the essence and basics of Feng Shui practice. It is mainly based on the fact that outside in the open there is plenty of highly vital Qi energy and oxygen (I'll tell you more about Qi in subsequent chapters).

Frequently Asked Questions about Feng Shui

Can Feng Shui affect me even though I am not aware of it?
The answer is "Yes!"

Would Feng Shui work for me even though I don't believe in it?
The answer is "Yes!"

Can Feng Shui improve my health, my relationships, my wealth and my life in general?
The answer is "Yes!"

Is it easy to learn Feng Shui?
The answer is "Yes, if you have a good teacher."

As soon as walls and roofs have been erected, 70 to 80 per cent of this vital energy (as well as the oxygen) is blocked and cannot enter the building. When business buildings and offices are designed according to Feng Shui principles, people can perform better, resulting in higher productivity and increased profitability. Businesses in shopping centers are also more successful when Feng Shui principles have been implemented. This has been proven by many examples.

Feng Shui offers techniques to draw more Qi energy and oxygen into the rooms and to improve the quality of air. This provides many benefits:

› *Your vitality is strengthened and you are able to sustain or improve your performance.*

› *You are more in harmony with your workplace. Your stress is reduced and this in turn improves your intuitive ability to make decisions.*

› *Your emotions are more balanced and you are happier and more positive in your outlook.*

› *You improve your relationships with your work colleagues, customers and family members.*

› *You enhance your prosperity consciousness, and have more abundance.*

› *Your health and longevity are enhanced.*

Multinational companies use Feng Shui

Business Feng Shui consultants in the West are often confronted by the dilemma of whether to give the names of companies that have successfully applied Feng Shui practices. Like other business consultancy services, references are often not easy to come by because of the need to maintain client confidentiality. However, the companies listed below have already received press coverage. They have designed their buildings according to Feng Shui principles or use Business Feng Shui services regularly:

> *the world headquarters of the Hong Kong and Shanghai Bank, Hong Kong*

> *the new headquarters of British Airways, UK*

> *the headquarters of the Donald Trump Group, New York, USA*

> *Siemens*

> *IBM*

> *the Virgin Group*

> *the Hyatt Hotel Group*

> *the Shangri-la Hotel Group*

> *the Holiday Inn Group*

Millionaires intuitively practice Feng Shui

I have visited more than two hundred residences and business premises owned by multimillionaires in twenty countries. Guided by their intuition, these super rich people were able to select exceptionally good, high-energy Feng Shui locations in which to build their homes and establish their businesses.

The question I often asked them was, "Why did you select this location and not another?" The answer almost invariably came back: "It felt good at the time," or "I had a strong gut feeling about it."

From my observations, several factors that facilitate millionaires are revealed in the selection of good sites. The following situations stand out prominently:

> *The homes of the rich are most often near a lake, a bay, or an area abundant with fresh water.*

> *The water sites are on protected high ground with plenty of green areas.*

> *There are plenty of open green areas, particularly in front of the sites.*

> *The internal spaces and rooms of their homes are usually bright and cheerful.*

> *The selected areas have highly vitalized land and environmental energies, and low crime rates.*

Business is subtle warfare

Business is actually a subtle war you have to "fight" on many fronts. In running a successful modern business many skills are required, making it more complicated than real warfare. Warfare is considered successful when there are few casualties and minimal costs involved. Similarly, running a very successful business should involve few highly qualified employees and the lowest possible costs to ensure a good return.

In this "business warfare" there is a fundamental difference between Western and Asian perceptions of problem solving. While Westerners are used to adopting the "big stick" aggressive approach, Asians often adopt subtle Taoist strategies. A give-and-take approach is pursued, which may delay a project. Westerners have generally — and wrongly — mistaken this subtle approach for a weakness in decision making. This is not so.

These two different approaches to solving business problems can be illustrated when comparing Western boxing with Chinese Tai Chi (sometimes translated as "shadow boxing"). In boxing you use all your strength to knock down your opponent, with the result that you lose lots of energy and both you and your opponent get hurt. In Tai Chi, soft movements are applied where you make use of your opponent's strength to weaken him. In this way you find an opportunity to overcome your opponent by attacking his weakest position. When there is a fight between a boxer and a seasoned Tai Chi practitioner, irrespective of body size, I always bet on the Tai Chi practitioner because I know his or her chance of winning is excellent.

Tai Chi is a Taoist practice and so is Feng Shui. Taoism is based on the writings of Chinese philosopher Lao-tzu, who advocated humility. It is about working with the forces of the universe rather than working against them or trying to control them. Both Tai Chi and Feng Shui practice apply natural laws and smooth, vitalized energy and subtlety to overcome adversity. In fact the same laws apply when running a business. The less effort and expenditure you apply, the better off you are. The Chinese, Japanese and Koreans who subscribe to Taoist practice consciously apply this non-aggressive way of conducting their businesses. These subtle practices comprise the following strategies:

Taoist strategies in business

1. Prolonging a negotiation to observe what the customer or opponent really wants; studying their strengths and weaknesses to facilitate decision making.
2. Behaving in a way that makes you appear to be weak. When an opportunity arises, "a mouse can overcome an elephant."

3. Using the least effort or funding by networking, and/or forming alliances and partnerships to handle large or complicated business deals.
4. Copying a competitor's products and innovating your own to save time and cost. Continually innovating to satisfy and keep customers.
5. Seeing everybody as a potential customer.
6. Always being polite and providing first-rate service at all times with a smile. The customer is always right!
7. Having a flexible approach, bending with the wind like a bamboo plant to accommodate changing conditions.
8. Living and working in harmony with your community and your environment — the practice of Feng Shui!

Asians, especially the Chinese, apply all of these eight practices. That is why they are so successful. The fifty million overseas Chinese who spread around the world are a very successful group of entrepreneurs. In the Asian countries, where they are also present outside of China in large numbers, they have a substantial interest in the local economies.

The Chinese are so successful in the Asian "dragon countries" (such as Malaysia, Thailand and Indonesia), that the question, "What made them so successful?" is often asked in Western countries. The answer is: They adopt all eight of the subtle practices listed above and practice Feng Shui as part of their culture daily. They may be temporarily affected by economic downturn cycles, but with the practice of Feng Shui recovery is usually very rapid.

The scope of Business Feng Shui
Business Feng Shui can be defined as the selection and design of healthy, harmonious and vitalized working spaces, furniture and symbols that maintain an ideal state of harmony and balance in both the microsphere and macrosphere environments to promote peak performance and success.

Modern Business Feng Shui, however, has a much wider scope that could be described by the key words "space organization," "geobiology" and "environmental study." Here are some examples of how it can be implemented:

1. harmonious building design to enhance selling and renting;

2. vitalized house/apartment design to enhance healthy living and working;

3. office layout for effective and enhanced staff performance;

4. vitalized workplace layout to improve productivity

5. *applied Business Feng Shui to revive unprofitable companies;*

6. *building ecology (e.g., identification of toxins in buildings);*

7. *geomancy — identification of negative and positive earth energies to eliminate health problems in homes and offices;*

8. *energetic power places identified and utilized;*

9. *preventative health care for office executives and managers;*

10. *Feng Shui as health therapy for "sick" buildings;*

11. *environmental study of inside the building;*

12. *environmental study of what is outside the building;*

13. *work study to reduce costs;*

14. *powerful business logo design;*

15. *public parks and nature reserves designed to follow nature's laws;*

16. *town and city design for business success and growth;.*

17. *design for the revitalization/rejuvenation of towns and cities;*

18. *design of power places;*

19. *design of rock gardens, water gardens and Zen gardens;*

20. *design of water fountains and waterfalls;*

21. *geopuncture to neutralize negative and toxic surface and underground energies.*

In view of the diversity of these aspects, the complexity of the field of Business Feng Shui becomes obvious. It is not just about moving furniture or changing room design, but about deeper research comprising the study of landscape, building, humans, and their interaction. The expertise is in knowing how to evaluate and connect these many factors. Positive structures have to be strengthened and problems identified. Then suitable remedies are selected.

Modern Business Feng Shui also integrates the aspects of geobiology and building biology. A Feng Shui remedy such as the calculation of the best compass direction for the optimum workplace of a certain individual will not be effective if this person is sitting on a geopathic stress field — for example, a water line — and is exposed to heavy amounts of toxins or electrosmog. Only when certain priorities have been considered do the more subtle auspicious energies have a supportive effect.

Reading the next chapters will give you the opportunity to look at your company from a new perspective. Not only your personal performance and commitment counts, but also the outer structures and the environment. The building you occupy is like your "second skin" and has a considerable effect on your life and your success.

As you read this book you will find many indications as to why, for example, you feel very comfortable or uncomfortable in your office. Maybe you have been thinking of moving your desk for a long time. Or you want to design a new logo. Questions such as "Why has this talk or interview been successful? Or not?" can be further explained by looking at aspects of the room in which it took place.

When you sharpen your eyes and check your store entrance or the location and design of other buildings, you may find structures that are strengthening or weakening you.

Last but not least, Business Feng Shui provides you with an insight into the Asian way of thinking and acting, which may lead to a deeper understanding of your business partners and greater competitiveness.

The next chapter will give you an overview of the different aspects and disciplines of Feng Shui.

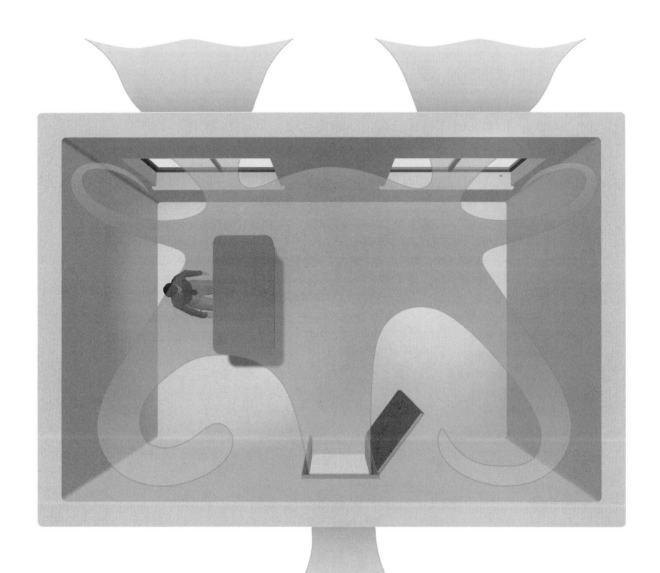

Energy flow

CHAPTER 2
Feng Shui Practice — An Overview

Although most of the basic principles in Home Feng Shui and Business Feng Shui are similar, many of their practical applications are vastly different. Basically, a home is our sanctuary, the place where we live a tranquil, secluded life and feel protected together with our loved ones and family. It is a place where we rest and regain our energy. We do not want outside interference. Some homes are reinforced like a fortress, with high security fences and guard dogs patrolling the compound. "No Trespassing" signs are boldly displayed outside some houses.

A business environment is the opposite of a home environment. In business we spend millions trying to entice and persuade customers to come to our store or business or just call so that we can have an opportunity to make a sale. Customers give us business that then helps us to pay our bills, pay our rent and living expenses and make a profit for the future.

So, you can appreciate that there is a significant difference between a home and a business environment. Feng Shui practice has to be adapted to fit the competitive and proactive business environment, with the purpose of attracting as many customers as possible.

In the business world, five Feng Shui factors have priority:

› *Clean air and strongly vitalized Qi in the building*

› *A strong backing for the company building*

› *A stable building with a supportive environment*

Energy flow

Diagram 2.1: A well-designed room that allows cosmic Qi and oxygen to circulate evenly throughout the room while the stale air exits through the window.

> *Location in a harmonious environment or landscape*
> *A harmonious, relaxing interior design to attract customers and reduce work stress*

Let's look at some of the basics of Feng Shui.

Qi energy

Cosmic Qi is a subtle energy that gives life to all living things. According to the teachings of acupuncture, the vital energy Qi enters the body during birth and flows along the meridians. All body cells are connected by this energy flow. Acupuncturists put needles into certain points on the body to release blockages and rebalance the flow of Qi.

The procedure with buildings is similar — the design and fittings are studied and changed if necessary in order to improve the Qi flow. Because Qi and oxygen also follow the wind and moving water, we use plants and fountains, for example, in order to bring additional Qi and oxygen into the building. This will improve the quality of the air, which becomes fresh and vitalizing like the air in the open.

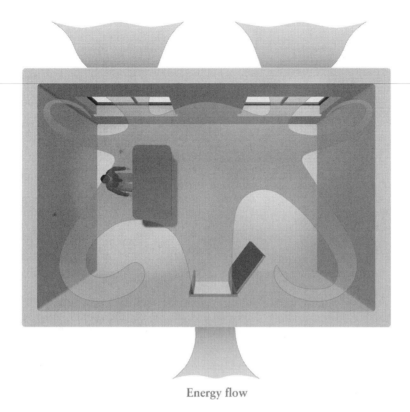

Energy flow

Diagram 2.2: This is also a well-designed office. The wall opposite the door diverts 70–80 per cent of cosmic energy and oxygen to circulate in the room, leaving only 20–30 per cent to escape.

Qi flow in rooms

The door of an office is like a person's mouth. It is the opening through which 70 to 80 per cent of cosmic energy and oxygen moves in; the remaining 20 to 30 per cent comes through the window. (Offices with no windows tend to have lower Qi energy and oxygen.)

The most important factor to consider when designing an office is to ensure that cosmic energy and oxygen are able to circulate to all areas of the room to ensure that its occupants are able to utilize the cosmic energy and oxygen before it exits.

The placement of doors and windows is therefore important. Many modern offices are designed with the door and window opposite each other. Cosmic energy and oxy-

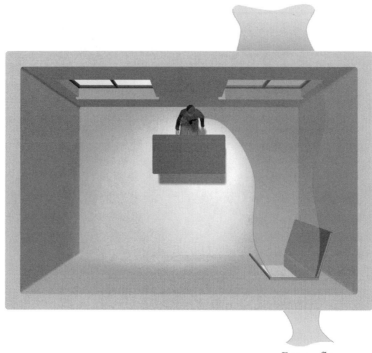

Energy flow

Diagram 2.3: Before the Qi can circulate evenly around the room, it is leaking through the window that is directly opposite the door. The result is fatigue, lack of concentration and poor work performance for the room's occupants.

gen leak out of these modern offices before they can circulate to other areas in a room. Diagram 2.1 shows an ideal office design that enables cosmic energy and oxygen to be retained much longer. A person working in an office as shown in Diagrams 2.1 and 2.2 receives more cosmic energy and oxygen and is more likely to be highly vitalized and able to perform better.

Water, an important factor for good Feng Shui

Moving water creates friction causing electromagnetic fields which attract more Qi and oxygen. The air becomes fresher.

In many respects, Europeans have already practiced Feng Shui for hundreds of years. Designers of historic buildings often used fountains and moving water pools in front entrances to enhance beneficial Qi and vitality. Many modern shopping malls and city squares now use various types of water fountains to attract people. Water facilities are important Feng Shui tools.

An indoor fountain in the office is a good Feng Shui remedy to attract more energy and oxygen into the room. For enclosed areas make sure that the fountain is correctly placed. Consider the size and shape as well as the harmony with the people working in that space (also see chapter 3).

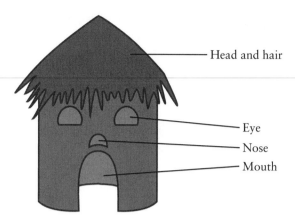

Diagram 2.4: This type of primitive house is still found in less developed areas like Africa, South America, Indonesia and Borneo.

Interaction between human and building

Through the long history of human evolution, our ancestors developed an indivisible link between themselves and their dwellings. They even built their homes with a full likeness to the human face and body. A house or a building became their protective cover against enemies and bad weather and other threatening conditions. It is a sanctuary where we feel safe, even though we may be less protected and more vulnerable in a glass-walled house or office.

We also select a house or business building that best resembles our personal taste and behavior. Two houses or business spaces may look alike from the outside, but are completely different in interior decor and fixtures that have been selected to suit the individual tastes of the occupants.

Once you select a house or a building, the design and character as well as the shape of the building takes over and controls you — it affects your behavior and your emotions. Diagram 2.6 is a house with a split roof that has been shown to cause disharmony amongst its occupants.

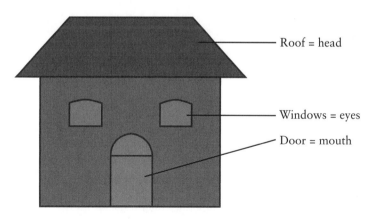

Diagram 2.5: Many modern houses also have the likeness of the human face.

A family may be a very harmonious one when it first moves into this building with a split roof. Over time, even though it can sometimes take up to three years or 72 moon cycles, the negative energy of the split roof completely affects the family members. Disharmony sets in, resulting in quarrels and separation, even divorce. In Zurich, Switzerland, a compatible couple divorced after living for six years in this house. They remarried after they both moved to another house.

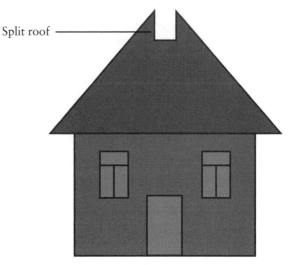

Split roof

Diagram 2.6: A house with a split roof.

The building reflects your health problems

You actually adopt the consciousness of the building, for it represents you. The roof of a house represents your head and hair; the walls represent your skin. The windows represent your eyes, the beam structures represent your skeleton and the door represents your mouth and nose, and so on.

In Malaysia there was a man who had a skin disease on his scalp and no doctor could treat him. I found that many roof tiles on his old house were broken and displaced in almost the exact locations as the diseased patches on his head. Re-roofing the house cured his hair and scalp problem.

In another incident a woman in Hamburg, Germany, had a skin disease on the left side of her body. Medical treatments only gave partial relief. English ivy covered most of the left wall of her house. The roots of the ivy had loosened some of the wall plaster, which was peeling off, just like her skin. Cutting down the ivy and replastering the wall allowed her skin to restore itself to good health.

These stories are not coincidences; they relate to observations according to Feng Shui criteria. I know enough cases to fill a book.

To prove that the inside wall of an office represents an occupant's skin, rub or scratch the office wall without letting the occupants know what you are doing. You will notice that the room's occupants, including yourself, become uncomfortable and weaker. By using the muscle test, an applied kinesiology technique, this body reaction can also be tested. This experiment has been done in more than ten countries, all with similar negative effects.

The Diagrams 2.7a–d below can best illustrate the close connection between humans and buildings. They also show that the shape of the floor plan affects the health and performance of the occupants.

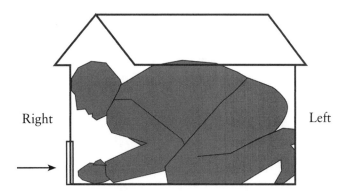

Diagram 2.7a: A house/building resembles a human body.

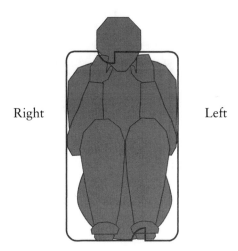

Diagram 2.7b: The building plan has been flipped over and is shown looking from the ground up ("basement perspective") with an outline of a human body superimposed onto a house/office floor plan.

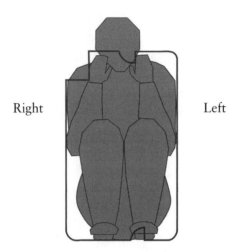

Right   Left

Diagram 2.7c: The back part of this office is missing. A weak backing means a lack of support in business. A business without strong support from customers, staff and banks has little chance of achieving success. Even with all its financial strength, a multinational company would be struggling to make a profit after moving into this office/building layout.

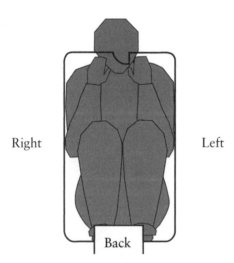

Right   Left

Back

Diagram 2.7d: The right-hand side of this office or building has a section missing. Occupants of this office/building would tend to have a higher incidence of right shoulder problems. Diagram 2.8 illustrates further connections with the Eight Aspirations. Each corner of a building or office room represents many attributes and phenomena in our daily life.

The Eight Life Aspirations

The Eight Life Aspirations, also called the Eight Life Situations, is one of the oldest Feng Shui systems. Diagram 2.8 shows the position of the aspiration in the whole building or in a single room that you may want to activate. Missing corners or wall areas will affect the respective aspiration. For example, if the Mentor or Helpful People area is missing, a company may find it difficult to obtain business loans and credit facilities from banks.

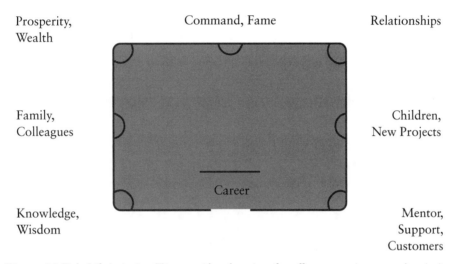

Prosperity, Wealth	Command, Fame	Relationships
Family, Colleagues	Career	Children, New Projects
Knowledge, Wisdom		Mentor, Support, Customers

Diagram 2.8: Eight Life Aspirations Trigrams with each section of an office representing a person's aspiration.

The East — West System

The ancient Chinese discovered more influences affecting a building positively or negatively. These are the energies in a room or building, or the energies generated by the room's features and structures. The ancients designed the Eight Trigrams Building System to guide builders in the selection of auspicious areas to locate a building on the land and to plan the rooms inside a building.

A format of the Eight Trigrams East-West System is set out in Diagram 2.9. The application of this system will be covered in chapters 9 and 10.

In Feng Shui practice we work with the Eight Trigrams of the East-West System, also called the Eight Mansions, in order to find the most auspicious room for the individual. The system of the Eight Trigrams shows a parallel to the basic symbol of life that is present in all the living cells of plants, animals and the human body (see Diagram 2.10a).

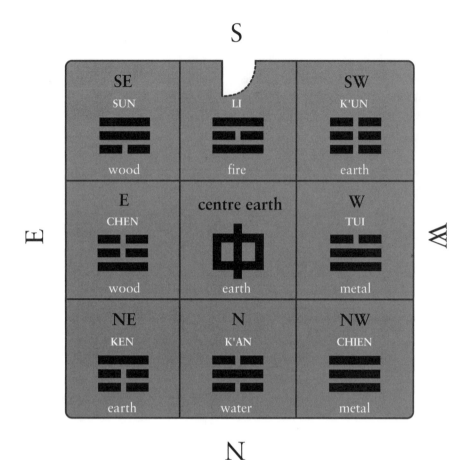

Diagram 2.9: A floor plan with the Later Heaven Eight Trigrams East-West System. The grids show the compass direction, the trigram name, the trigram symbol and the element.

The symbol of 8

The Eight Trigrams can be traced back to the symbol of 8. The outer halves of the 8 symbol sit on the side representing space for rooms/buildings, with the other inner half of the 8 in the middle to represent a central space to be shared by all the occupants (or staff) of the building. The Chinese call the inner central court the *Mingtang*.

The symbol of 8 is the well-known, ancient symbol of infinity. When you trace a figure 8 you cannot escape from it — it is a continuous flowing line. That is why 8 is also a symbol for harmony and prosperity.

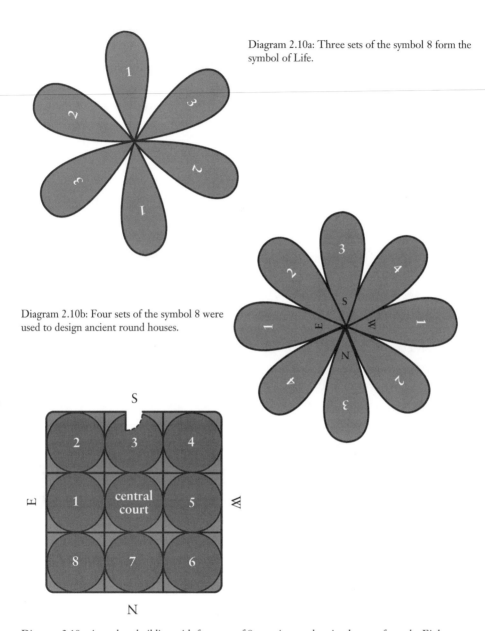

Diagram 2.10a: Three sets of the symbol 8 form the symbol of Life.

Diagram 2.10b: Four sets of the symbol 8 were used to design ancient round houses.

Diagram 2.10c: A modern building with four sets of 8 superimposed on its shape to form the Eight Trigrams East-West System. N.B.: The numbers 1 to 8 only illustrate the number of 8 symbols, namely eight, and have no other significance.

This is why in Hong Kong, Singapore, Thailand, Malaysia and Southern China a vehicle license plate with 88 or 888 commands several million US dollars. A lot of expensive cars registered in Germany often have one or more 8s on the license plates as well.

Studying and practicing Eight Trigrams Feng Shui is actually studying ourselves and how we interact with a building that then affects our cells, our behavior, our health and our performance.

The eight human energy spots

Recently, American and Australian health scientists have discovered that the subtle body's electromagnetic field is connected by eight vibrating energy spots (see Diagram 2.11a). These eight energy spots radiating from a human body are like human feelers touching the environment. These energy spots give a human the ability to feel the energy and surrounding conditions in a room or an open space. A negative or positive area in a room or a building invariably affects the occupant (see Diagram 2.11b).

Over time, when sitting and working in this room, the energies radiating from sharp corners of a cupboard or pillar will be perceived more or less consciously through the feelers. A person sitting in this room over a longer period of time would experience lower work performance. For this reason, indoor structures, fittings and fixtures should preferably have curved or rounded corners.

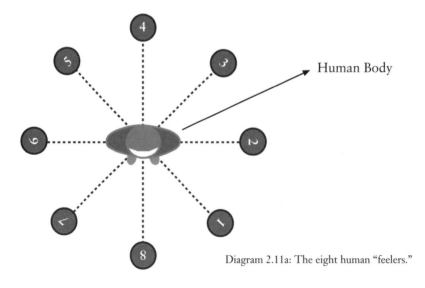

Human Body

Diagram 2.11a: The eight human "feelers."

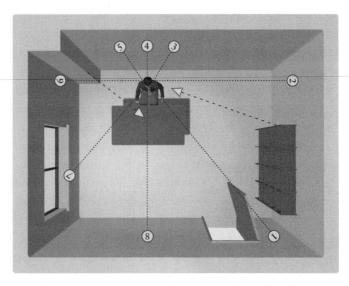

Diagram 2.11b: The human "feelers" can perceive the energies radiating from the sharp corners.

The location

Everything in nature — and we are part of nature — conforms to certain universal harmonic principles. Experience shows that there is a right time and place for everything to ensure exceptional success or fulfillment. We see plants grow luxuriously without human assistance. In spite of the best care and attention, we also see cultivated trees and plants that do not grow so well.

Similarly, when you operate a business or trade, you have to conform to nature's law when planning to improve your success. Feng Shui provides the ways to align with nature's law.

The human and business should be in harmony with the location. Not every business can flourish anywhere in a city or town. During my thirty years of experience as a corporate recovery consultant in Feng Shui, I discovered that a certain type of business can expand very fast in a certain sector or compass direction of a city.

Environmental conditions, landscape formations and population density are also factors that influence the location of a business. But even when you move a successful business into another sector, in spite of more favorable customer numbers and good infrastructure and facilities, it may not grow and prosper as well as you had planned. To establish a suitable location for a specific business or manufacturing concern, the services of an experienced Feng Shui consultant or geomancy expert should be sought.

Backing and Mingtang

As a building can be compared with the human body, the location should support the building. The back of the building should have a natural elevation such as a hill, a high wall or another building that provides a strong backing. The building and thus the company is protected from behind and, in a figurative sense, also receives support from the staff and shareholders, as well as outsiders such as the banks or the city council (also refer to chapter 6).

In the entrance area (the head area), there should be enough space for the building to breathe freely. The door is comparable to the mouth area, where most of the cosmic Qi and oxygen enters the building. This means that the entrance area should be open, big, and have no blocking or attacking structures. On the contrary, a narrow, winding entrance area has a "choking" effect and affects the good Qi flow within the building.

In Feng Shui we refer to the so-called Mingtang, meaning "bright hall" or "space." There is an inner Mingtang (the entrance area within the building), as well as an outer Mingtang (outside the building in the entrance area). For the Eight Trigrams in Diagram 2.10c, the central court of a building is also called Mingtang.

An old Feng Shui recommendation states that the square in front of the imperial palace should provide space for 100,000 horses. In modern times this means that there should be, if possible, a free and open space in front of an office building without obstruction by pillars, high walls or buildings close by. An auspicious outer Mingtang with an open view means not only that good energy can gather, but that people working there have the opportunity to develop more perspectives and "far-sightedness."

These basic rules for backing and Mingtang belong to the field of Landscape Feng Shui and have priority before all other disciplines, such as the East-West System and astrological factors.

Your personal compass directions

Feng Shui also considers the influence of the compass directions. Year after year, certain species of birds travel the same route from the northern hemisphere to the warmer southern hemisphere to avoid the cold winter. Similarly, every human is more or less in harmony with certain directions.

Not every compass direction in a city or town will suit you, even though your business may be sited in a very busy — and apparently auspicious — location. This Feng Shui harmony factor applies to owner-operators who have to personally run and manage a business. If you employ a manager, then the manager has to be in harmony, working both in your business and in your business location as well.

You should therefore know and use your best directions. The same principle is also applied inside the building. If you sit on the power spot of the office, you will get promoted more quickly. You will also be able to run your business more effectively and enjoy more respect.

Astrological factors

Feng Shui calculates astrological factors according to your birth date to help find your most harmonious and auspicious place to sit and sleep to recharge your energy and thus facilitate your work performance and become healthier. Certain planets, like Jupiter, radiate powerful frequencies towards Earth (see chapter 8). Some of these frequencies can cause fatigue if you sit facing their direction. The directions of the radiated frequencies from the planet change as it moves in its orbit. Feng Shui helps you to identify these negative rays so that you can avoid them.

On an advanced level there are the so-called Flying Stars astrological calculations which are only briefly mentioned in this book. By using the Flying Stars, predictions can be made — for example, which time period provides particularly auspicious energies supporting the prosperity of the company. Time periods of negative cosmic influences can also be identified, indicating the likelihood of more arguments, for example. Feng Shui remedies based on the Five Elements (chapter 3) may be used to counter these harmful effects. The Flying Stars are another dynamic time aspect that can be calculated for each month, each year, or longer time cycles.

Avoid negative energies

We are all continuously affected by negative or positive energies. Negative energy from geopathic stress rays caused by underground water is known to have caused cancer and other degenerative diseases. You must keep away from these harmful rays to be healthy and avoid chronic fatigue.

Furthermore, in modern offices we are affected by electrosmog caused by electrical wires, computers and office equipment. Without Feng Shui remedies the air is dry and stuffy. People working in such a stressful environment have difficulties concentrating and performing well. They suffer from headaches, lung problems and allergies more frequently. All these factors negatively affect productivity.

Some environments lack landscape vitality or are very aggressive to human habitation or business, causing health and business problems. With a good knowledge of Feng Shui you can identify these "black spots" to avoid needless suffering. Why handicap yourself unnecessarily in your work?

Many areas have bad underground energies called "black streams" (see chapter 13). Businesses located in such areas tend to have a higher incidence of failure. An experienced consultant can apply proven remedies to neutralize the negative effects so that businesses become successful again.

Planning and building according to Feng Shui

It is well known in Australia and Asia that residences that are built following Feng Shui principles are sold at ten to twenty per cent above market price. This presents a considerable advantage for developers and builders. Owners and investors also benefit because they have a building with high energy and comfortable living, which is easy to rent or sell.

The planning and construction of new buildings according to Feng Shui is another big field that cannot be covered by the scope of this book. The QI-MAG International Feng Shui and Geobiology Institute also teaches the principles of good design in buildings for architects, builders and interior designers. Refer to the appendix of this book for further information.

Business Feng Shui covers many more areas; this book can only cover a few of them. Feng Shui is an ancient science and art that gives respectable results and is practiced by two billion people worldwide. Be open enough to give it a try and feel the difference for yourself when you have implemented Feng Shui remedies. The information given in this book may give you some guidance, but it does not replace the advice of a trained Feng Shui consultant.

Use your intuition to guide you in the selection of a competent and experienced Feng Shui consultant and also check on their level of knowledge according to the twelve disciplines of Feng Shui.

The Twelve Disciplines of Feng Shui

1. *Cosmic Qi, oxygen and air quality*

2. *Yin and yang principles for harmony*

3. *The Five Elemental universal energies*

4. *Landscape Feng Shui, the study of the Four Celestial Animals Formation*

5. *The Eight Life Aspirations Trigrams in our daily life*

6. *The Earlier Heaven Trigrams (working with the spiritual realm)*

7. *The I-Qing Later Heaven Eight Trigrams, or the East — West System (location)*

8. The Lo'Shu Flying Stars System on time dimension (astrology and cosmology)

9. Geobiology and geomancy research into earth rays, cosmic and environmental energies

10. Identification and avoidance of working in locations with harmful radiations and negative frequencies (black spots)

11. Water and Mountain Dragon classics on water flows, water quality and mountain formations to enhance prosperity, abundance and posterity

12. Spiritual Feng Shui — the most advanced level to harness natural earth and cosmic Qi to empower human performance

CHAPTER 3
The Five Elements Principle

From their observations, ancient Taoist masters and sages discovered that everything on Planet Earth — whether naturally existing or man-made — could be attributed to a certain element. A group of five elements evolved: Water, Wood, Fire, Earth and Metal.

This elemental classification has a history of about 3000 years. Other old cultures, like the Indian, Egyptian and South American and Celtic cultures, classified objects and energies into four elements, namely Water, Air, Earth and Fire. These four elements are similar in application to the Chinese elements. Each group of elements is defined by its color, shape, structure, sound, energy type, taste, body organs, body types, seasons, time, etc.

When the Five Elements of Feng Shui come together they can positively affect, destroy, or drain each other. It is therefore important to understand the interaction of the elements in the three basic cycles.

The Three Basic Cycles of the Five Elements

1. The productive cycle

This cycle shows the positive, productive or birth-giving cycle when one element is giving birth and nourishing the following element. Wood nourishes Fire, Fire creates Earth, Metals can be found in the Earth, Metal can become liquid like Water, Water nourishes Wood.

2. *The destructive cycle*

In the destructive cycle one element is destroying another. Wood breaks up Earth, Earth sucks Water, Water destroys Fire, Fire melts Metal, Metal cuts Wood.

Only in exceptional cases of Feng Shui remedies is an element applied to destroy another element. Otherwise elements destroying each other should not be combined. For instance, if the elements Metal and Wood are used as the colors gold and green immediately next to each other (metal cuts wood), subtle turbulence is created that should be avoided in the workplace.

3. *The mother-and-child cycle*

It is common practice to apply this third, subtle elemental cycle if we wish to reduce or neutralize the harmful effects of a controlling element. This principle works on the basis that children drain a mother's energy.

For example, if a wall is painted blue (Water element), we select the element according to the mother-and-child cycle which can reduce a possible negative effect of the strong Water element. In this case we would use green shades (Wood element) for the other walls or furniture.

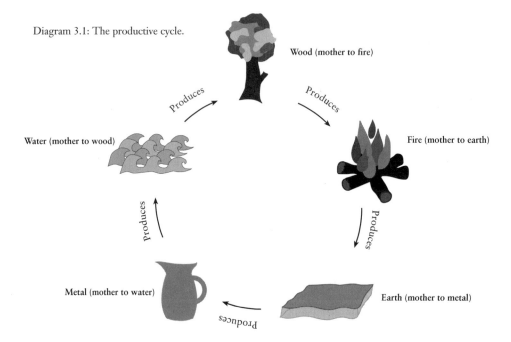

Diagram 3.1: The productive cycle.

Wood (mother to fire)

Produces

Produces

Water (mother to wood)

Fire (mother to earth)

Produces

Produces

Metal (mother to water)

Earth (mother to metal)

Produces

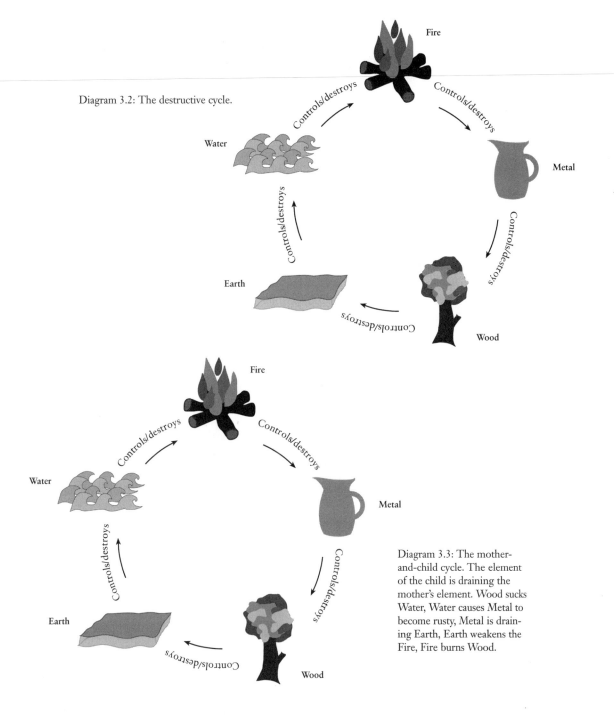

Diagram 3.2: The destructive cycle.

Diagram 3.3: The mother-and-child cycle. The element of the child is draining the mother's element. Wood sucks Water, Water causes Metal to become rusty, Metal is draining Earth, Earth weakens the Fire, Fire burns Wood.

The Energy Movements and Shapes of the Five Elements

Water element

The Water element is nourished by the Metal, destroyed by Earth, and weakened by Wood. The shape or movement of Water energy is wavy or step-shaped and is moving downwards and spreading towards the sides. Water has a cooling and blending energy. The color of water is blue.

For industries where heat and fire are used in manufacturing, as in a foundry or plastics factory, it is important to avoid buildings that have a Water roof and have their walls painted blue. The cooling Water energy would weaken the business and affect the functioning of the machines. I have seen business failures in New Zealand, Malaysia and Germany connected with this problem.

Remedy — in this case the destroying element of the Water, Earth, would have to be used. Use beige and light brown colors on the walls and on the ceilings of a Water element building as a remedy.

Diagram 3.4a: The movement of water is down and towards the sides (condensation).

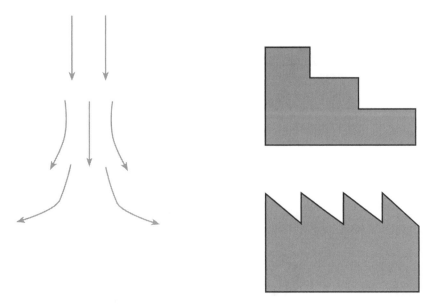

Diagram 3.4b: Water element buildings.

Wood element

The Wood element is nourished by Water, destroyed by Metal, and weakened by Fire.

The energy of Wood is expanding in all directions like a tree in spring. The Wood element shape is long, tall and narrow. The color of wood is green.

As the Wood energy is drained by the Fire, care needs to be taken when designing a Wood shape building, to ensure that many buildings around the construction site do not have Fire roofs. The Wood shape building would be drained which would adversely affect its occupants.

Diagram 3.5a: The Wood energy is expanding in all directions.

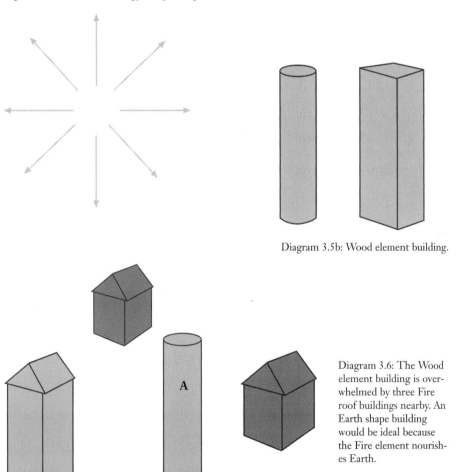

Diagram 3.5b: Wood element building.

Diagram 3.6: The Wood element building is overwhelmed by three Fire roof buildings nearby. An Earth shape building would be ideal because the Fire element nourishes Earth.

Fire element

The Fire element is nourished by Wood, destroyed by Water, and weakened by Earth. Fire energy is ascending. Fire shapes are sharp and "aggressive." Fire colors are red, pink, maroon, purple and violet.

The steep Fire roof (saddle roof) creates an upward pull of energy that draws stale hot air and Qi energy up to the roof, thereby giving a cooling effect to the ground level or lower floors of a building during hot weather. A high-pitched Fire roof is in fact not suitable for cold or temperate climates. If a Fire roof is required in areas where there are heavy snowfalls, a low-pitched roof may be an alternative.

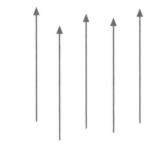

Diagram 3.7a: Upward-moving Fire energy.

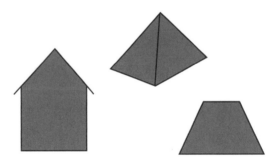

Diagram 3.7b: Fire element building shapes.

Earth element

The Earth element is nourished by Fire, destroyed by Wood, and weakened by Metal. Earth energy moves horizontally to and fro, creating spaces for the roots of trees to penetrate. As a result, earth is able to absorb large quantities of water. The Earth shape is level or flat on top; colors are brown, yellow, orange and beige.

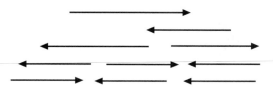

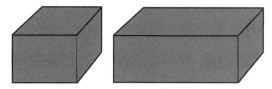

Diagram 3.8a: Movement of Earth energy.

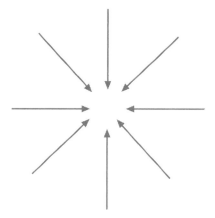

Diagram 3.8b: Buildings that have an Earth shape.

Metal element

The Metal element is nourished by Earth, destroyed by Fire, and weakened by Water. Metal energy, which moves inwards from all directions, is the complete opposite of Wood energy. The shape of the Metal element is a curve or dome. The colors of Metal are gold and silver. White looks like silver and is sometimes used to represent Metal. White is actually a neutral color, representing all the seven spectrum colors of the rainbow.

Diagram 3.9a: Energy of Metal.

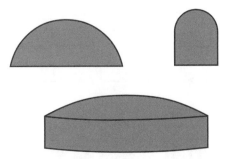

Diagram 3.9b: Buildings with a Metal shape.

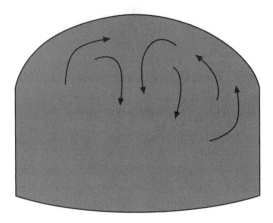

Diagram 3.9c: A Metal element curved roof redirects energy downwards and is ideal for retaining heat and energy.

The influence of an elemental energy on a person

Every person can have several elements — for example, according to their character, body constitution, birth year or Personal Life Trigram.

In Feng Shui two elements are especially considered: the birth year element, which is important if Feng Shui remedies have to be implemented, and the Personal Life Trigram, which has to be considered for the ratings of the East-West System and the design of a personal company logo.

In the table that follows you will find your birth year element. For example, a person born between February 19, 1901, and February 7, 1902, is a Metal Ox person. The combination of an element and an animal sign provides certain typical characteristics of a person.

Table 1: Chinese Calendar with Birth Year Element and Astrological Animal Symbols

Year	Element	Animal	Year	Element	Animal
19.02.1901	Metal	Ox	27.01.1941	Metal	Snake
08.02.1902	Water	Tiger	15.01.1942	Water	Horse
29.01.1903	Water	Hare	05.02.1943	Water	Sheep
16.02.1904	Wood	Dragon	25.01.1944	Wood	Monkey
04.02.1905	Wood	Snake	13.02.1945	Wood	Rooster
25.01.1906	Fire	Horse	02.02.1946	Fire	Dog
13.02.1907	Fire	Sheep	22.01.1947	Fire	Boar
02.02.1908	Earth	Monkey	10.02.1948	Earth	Rat
22.01.1909	Earth	Rooster	29.01.1949	Earth	Ox
10.02.1910	Metal	Dog	17.02.1950	Metal	Tiger
30.01.1911	Metal	Boar	06.02.1951	Metal	Hare
18.02.1912	Water	Rat	27.01.1952	Water	Dragon
06.02.1913	Water	Ox	14.02.1953	Water	Snake
26.01.1914	Wood	Tiger	03.02.1954	Wood	Horse
14.02.1915	Wood	Hare	24.01.1955	Wood	Sheep
03.02.1916	Fire	Dragon	12.02.1956	Fire	Monkey
23.01.1917	Fire	Snake	31.01.1957	Fire	Rooster
11.02.1918	Earth	Horse	18.02.1958	Earth	Dog
01.02.1919	Earth	Sheep	08.02.1959	Earth	Boar
20.02.1920	Metal	Monkey	28.01.1960	Metal	Rat
08.02.1921	Metal	Rooster	15.02.1961	Metal	Ox
28.01.1922	Water	Dog	05.02.1962	Water	Tiger
16.02.1923	Water	Boar	25.01.1963	Water	Hare
05.02.1924	Wood	Rat	13.02.1964	Wood	Dragon
25.01.1925	Wood	Ox	02.02.1965	Wood	Snake
13.02.1926	Fire	Tiger	21.01.1966	Fire	Horse
02.02.1927	Fire	Hare	09.02.1967	Fire	Sheep
23.01.1928	Earth	Dragon	30.01.1968	Earth	Monkey
10.02.1929	Earth	Snake	17.02.1969	Earth	Rooster
30.01.1930	Metal	Horse	06.02.1970	Metal	Dog
17.02.1931	Metal	Sheep	27.01.1971	Metal	Boar
06.02.1932	Water	Monkey	15.02.1972	Water	Rat
26.01.1933	Water	Rooster	03.02.1973	Water	Ox
14.02.1934	Wood	Dog	23.01.1974	Wood	Tiger
04.02.1935	Wood	Boar	11.02.1975	Wood	Hare
24.01.1936	Fire	Rat	31.01.1976	Fire	Dragon
11.02.1937	Fire	Ox	18.02.1977	Fire	Snake
31.01.1938	Earth	Tiger	07.02.1978	Earth	Horse
19.02.1939	Earth	Hare	28.01.1979	Earth	Sheep
08.02.1940	Metal	Dragon	16.02.1980	Metal	Monkey

Year	Element	Animal
05.02.1981	Metal	Rooster
25.01.1982	Water	Dog
13.02.1983	Water	Boar
02.02.1984	Wood	Rat
20.02.1985	Wood	Ox
09.02.1986	Fire	Tiger
29.01.1987	Fire	Hare
17.02.1988	Earth	Dragon
06.02.1989	Earth	Snake
27.01.1990	Metal	Horse
15.02.1991	Metal	Sheep
04.02.1992	Water	Monkey
23.01.1993	Water	Rooster
10.02.1994	Wood	Dog
31.01.1995	Wood	Boar
19.02.1996	Fire	Rat
07.02.1997	Fire	Ox
28.01.1998	Earth	Tiger
16.02.1999	Earth	Hare
05.02.2000	Metal	Dragon
24.01.2001	Metal	Snake
12.02.2002	Water	Horse
01.02.2003	Water	Sheep
22.01.2004	Wood	Monkey
09.02.2005	Wood	Rooster
29.01.2006	Fire	Dog
18.02.2007	Fire	Boar
02.02.2008	Earth	Rat
26.01.2009	Earth	Ox
14.01.2010	Metal	Tiger
03.02.2011	Metal	Hare
23.01.2012	Water	Dragon
10.02.2013	Water	Snake
31.01.2014	Wood	Horse
19.02.2015	Wood	Sheep
08.02.2016	Fire	Monkey
28.01.2017	Fire	Rooster
16.02.2018	Earth	Dog
05.02.2019	Earth	Boar
25.01.2020	Metal	Rat

The application of the Five Elements

It is recommended that business premises for the twenty-first century be painted with bright, cheerful colors to stimulate and relax the eyes. Cheerful colors also reduce fatigue and depression, especially during the winter months in colder countries.

Before you decide on a new color scheme for your office, it is in your best interest to employ an interior designer or Feng Shui consultant who has a good knowledge of the Five Elements Principle. If the elements are harmonically matching with the individuals using the office, it is possible to improve well-being and work performance and avoid possible health problems.

In choosing colors for individuals in an office, care needs to be exercised to ensure that the right colors, shapes and fittings are selected. The basic rule is: every person can "take" natural wood — for example, as furniture or wall panels — as well as harmonic patterns in pastel colors or white.

An individual should be surrounded by supporting (productive cycle) or neutral colors. Combinations of the destructive cycle should be avoided.

It is also possible that a person has a preference for their conflicting element. This may be caused by an imbalance of the body constitution or a short-term requirement of the body in a certain situation. Example: A Water element person may like the color brown. Maybe he or she needs this color to strengthen his/her grounding and balance.

It is very important to distinguish between temporary color requirements and the long-term color design of a room. The room should be designed to match the birth year element, as a conflicting element will have a weakening effect after only a few weeks. Short-term element requirements can be met with colored clothing or decorations such as pictures, cushions or vases in the appropriate color.

Birth year elemental conflict

However, these personal birth year elemental conflicts with other colors or objects are only applicable for a person when in an enclosed office or inside a building. In an open space environment, these birth year conflicts and draining cycles do not apply. This is because in the open space we are part of the environment and as such are also affected by other natural energies. Therefore the overpowering energies of the controlling elements have only a minimal effect.

Example: A Wood element person should use the following colors: Water — blue (nourishing), Wood — green (neutral) and white (neutral), or a little bit of Earth (this element is controlled by the Wood). An indoor fountain (Water) or a plant (Wood) are also supportive, whereas the colors gold and silver (Metal element), as well as metal objects, should be two yards away from the body (see Diagram 3.10).

Please note: Never paint your wall purple or violet (Fire element). These two colors over-activate the head energy causing an overactive pineal gland, which in turn results in health problems.

A light blue color has an antiseptic effect. It can be specially recommended for hospitals and clinics and will help to reduce the need for detergents and toxic disinfectants. The use of multiple colors and cheerful color schemes together with healthy plants in hospital wards facilitate self-healing and a faster recovery for patients. Shades of gray or dull mundane colors are to be avoided at all costs.

The color of clothing

Clothing can quickly be changed and matched with the current requirements of the person. Therefore we should not be confused by an Earth element person wearing green for a while, which is actually a conflicting color. In the case of clothing this color may represent a time of personal growth and progress.

The color red has a strongly activating effect and gives extra energy. Purple and violet (Fire element) should not be worn over a longer period of time as they activate the head area too much, which affects the grounding of the person.

When a person prefers beige and brown shades, they want to ground themselves. It is also possible to do this by eating a lot; however it is better to select colors with a

Diagram 3.10:
Color scheme for
a Wood element
person.

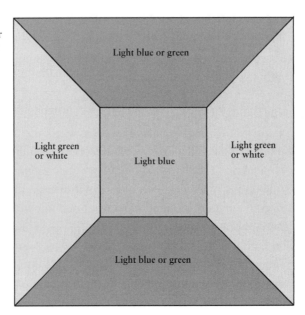

Case Study

The offices of a very successful small company in Munich, Germany, were enlarged, renovated and repainted. The interior designer did not know about the Feng Shui Five Elements Principle. The office walls of the chief executive were painted with light brown (Earth) and light pink (Fire) but the carpet was dark blue (Water). After the renovation the boss, who was born in a Fire year, suffered daily from chronic fatigue and was forced to work from home.

The problem was the dark blue carpet destroying his Fire and strongly weakening him. Putting a large green carpet (Wood) under his table to strengthen him solved the problem. At the same time the room's blue carpet (Water) strengthened the green carpet (Wood). The boss's seating location was also moved away from the light brown wall (Earth) that drained his Fire element. His health improved and he now works with more energy than ever before.

grounding effect. Yellow also belongs to the Earth element and enhances your mental ability.

The Metal element is represented by gold- or silver-colored clothing or jewelry and strengthens willpower. The color blue represents the Water element as well as prosperity, movement and travel.

Whatever colorful clothing you decide to wear should be based on your intuitive feeling at the time. Maybe your seven energy centers (chakras) or your body's constitutional elements during a specific period need to be reinforced by a certain color or several colors.

You should never wear a certain color exclusively just because a glamorous model or famous designer recommends it. In fact, never wear gray or black during the day. Black is the contrary of white — it lacks the seven colors of the rainbow which give life to the body. Black makes people feel more depressed, suppresses the body energy and expresses inner grief.

Table 2: Your Supporting or Neutral Elements at Your Workplace

Your birth year element	Colors supporting you	Examples for decorations
Wood	blue, green, white	fountain, waterfall picture, plant
Fire	green, red, pink, maroon, white	plants, red objects
Earth	red, pink, maroon, brown, beige, yellow, orange, white	rocks, earthenware, ceramics, red objects
Metal	brown, beige, yellow, orange, gold, silver, white	earthenware, ceramics, rocks, metal objects
Water	gold, silver, blue, white	fountains, waterfall pictures, metal objects

Table 3: Elements To Avoid in Your Immediate Working Environment

Your birth year element	Colors to be avoided	Decorations to be avoided
Wood	gold, silver	metal objects
Fire	blue	fountains and waterfall pictures
Earth	green	plants
Metal	red, purple, violet, pink, maroon	red objects
Water	brown, beige, yellow, orange	earth-colored ceramics, rocks

CHAPTER 4
A Company's Name and Logo

A company's name and logo are important factors that substantially contribute to the success or failure of a company. When selecting a name or designing a logo, a number of important Feng Shui rules should therefore be considered.

The vibration of the company's name
From my work with many "sick companies" I have discovered that a good name contributes substantially to the company's success and ability to survive. Why? As a symbol and vibration, the name of a company represents the totality of the business. Just as your face and the way you behave represents you — your trademark — a good name creates a positive vibrational energy and sound that is like well-composed music.

We are all affected by symbols and sounds. It is the sound or mantra of a powerful company that attracts people and is associated with success. Usually people do not like to be associated with failure or weakness.

Famous names
A powerful name should have a continuous high pitch from the beginning to the end, or at the beginning and end. The names Toyota and McDonalds are excellent examples that represent two successful companies in their field, both having a harmonious high-pitched sound from beginning to end. The vibration of the name should move up gradually, and is likened to a successful company that performs well year after year.

A name that rises continuously is not a suitable name. A company is like a person; it cannot rise or make continuous progress without a pause for rest. This is unrealistic. A name that rises continuously has a short lifespan.

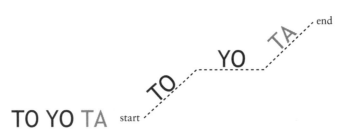

Diagram 4.1: Sound diagram for the name Toyota.

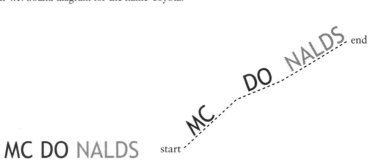

Diagram 4.2: Sound diagram for the name McDonalds.

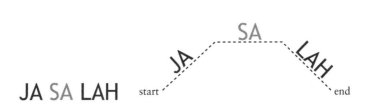

Diagram 4.3: Sound diagram for the name Jasalah.

If there is a long leveling of the sound tone, it indicates the company would face a period of stagnation that would weaken its performance. Furthermore, the leveling tone is too long, making it too negative for a company name.

Let us examine a company by the name of *Jasalah* that has become bankrupt in Indonesia. *Lah* sounds like a person lacking in vitality and stamina. The name of a company represents the total consciousness of a business. If the name lacks vitality and stamina, then this company will not be able to sustain its position for long. Customers will intuitively not deal with a weak company. *Lah* at the end is like a person running a race but lacking the stamina to finish the race and win. In Indonesian *salah* means wrong, which is also negative.

Harmony of the business name

Apart from the importance of having a strong tone for the name of a company, the name has to be in harmony with the business or the main business, if a company is involved in many types of business or trade. According to my research the name Toyota is 95 per cent in harmony with the vehicle business. The name McDonalds is 91 per cent in harmony with selling hamburgers made from beef, but is not in harmony with selling chicken or fish burgers. The name Pizza Hut is only about 70 per cent in harmony with selling pizzas. Obviously, this weaker harmony would affect the performance of Pizza Hut.

The company's logo

A logo represents the core image and essence of a company. The trademark is the nucleus that acts as a catalyst. It determines how the company's founder, its employees and the public perceive and recognize the company.

A company logo should stand out prominently, and powerfully project its symbolic quality. We can see that some company logos project powerful, magnetic and vibrant energy, while other logos are mundane, weak and have no vitality.

The Mercedes symbol of the trinity within a circle is a powerful symbol that attracts people's attention to it. The original IBM symbol also had that attracting quality.

The Olympic symbol of five rings linked together, representing the unity of five continents, is another very auspicious symbol. The popularity of the Olympic Games could not even be spoiled by the dubious activities of some members of their top organization.

The designing of company logos is a lucrative business, and could be even more so for those who understand the power of symbols. Unfortunately, more than 70 per cent of company logos, especially those in the West, tend to break most of the Feng Shui designing rules.

You can also use a pendulum or applied kinesiology techniques (muscle testing) to determine whether your company's name and logo are in harmony with your business. You may want to consult an applied kinesiologist or a dowsing expert to help you check.

General guidelines for good logo design

The following basic guidelines can help you to avoid some pitfalls in logo design:

> *Logos or trademarks should represent a trading field, profession, goods/tools, the corporate vision or the target group.*

> *Logos or trademarks may also depict the initials of a company, group or individual.*

> *A special symbol or place may be used as a logo/trademark — for example, the kiwi bird representing products from New Zealand.*

> *Logos should stand out. They should be simple, plain and easy to remember.*

> *Logos need to conform to the Five Elements Principle in both design and color scheme (see previous chapter). Select the colors from the Five Elements that are in harmony with the owner's Personal Life Trigram.*

> *For a family-run business, the shape of the logo, which is attributed to a certain element, should be in harmony with the Personal Life Trigram element of the owner.*

> *Never use your family's coat of arms as a logo, as it not only represents your company but also your whole family; this makes you more open to attacks.*

> *Homogeneous or balanced shapes are harmonious.*

> *Shapes should not be threatening; they should look neutral or attractive.*

> *Round or curved shapes are preferred. If possible avoid sharp, pointed and angular shapes.*

> *All sharp, pointed arrow shapes or triangular shapes are negative, unless enclosed in a circle or square. The sharp points must touch the frame line.*

> *All sharp, pointed arrow shapes that are pointing horizontally are less negative than those pointing downwards.*

> *The circle represents the earth and the universe. Never break the line of a circle or semicircle.*

> *Lines or colored areas should not become paler towards the outside as the company would also "fade out."*

> *Continuous lines are preferable to broken or pale lines.*

Basic logo shapes and the Five Elements Principle

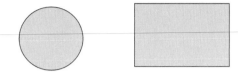

Diagram 4.4: Earth element shapes.

Diagram 4.5: Metal element shapes.

Diagram 4.6: Water element shapes.

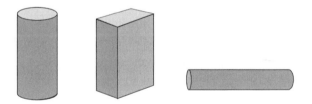

Diagram 4.7: Wood element shapes.

Diagram 4.8: Fire element shapes.

Let us recall the strengthening cycle, as shown in Diagram 4.9 below:

WATER ▶▶ WOOD ▶▶ FIRE ▶▶ EARTH ▶▶ METAL ▶▶ WATER

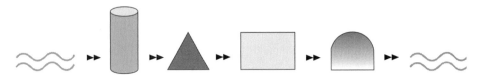

Diagram 4.9: Elements of the strengthening cycle in harmony (the double arrow indicates possible combinations).

Let us check once again on the conflict cycle, with the elements weakening each other:

WATER =/= FIRE =/= METAL =/= WOOD =/= EARTH =/= WATER

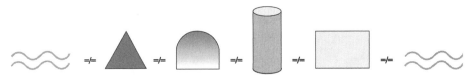

Diagram 4.10: Elements in conflict, weakening or destroying each other.

Examples for logo design

For these logo examples, symbols of the Five Elements were combined with each other: Earth (E) = circle, Metal (M) = semicircle, Water (W) = wave shape, Wood (WD) = long slim rectangular shape, Fire (F) = triangle shape or sharp points. $\vee$ = positive, X = negative. The logo color should be in harmony with the company.

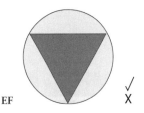

EF $\vee$ X

Diagram 4.11a: Although elements are in harmony, the triangle pointing downwards is negative for a business.

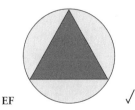

EF $\vee$

Diagram 4.11b: The direction of this triangle is auspicious.

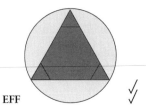

EFF

Diagram 4.11c: Earth with a lot of Fire — the big triangle is subdivided into smaller triangles.

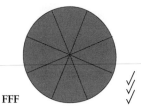

FFF

Diagram 4.11d: Fire-triangles, harmoniously arranged in a circle.

EFW

Diagram 4.11e: Very disharmonious due to the Fire–Water conflict.

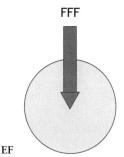

FFF

Diagram 4.11f: Although the elements are in harmony, the arrow pointing down is inauspicious. Furthermore, the circle is broken.

EF

MM

Diagram 4.11g: Negative — the circle is split into two.

MM

Diagram 4.11h: The circle is split into two halves but is connected at the bottom so that it still symbolizes unity.

E

Diagram 4.11i: The dotted line indicates weakness and a lack of confidence. It is therefore inauspicious for a logo.

E

Diagram 4.11j: A continuous circle line is positive. The initials of the company may be placed in the center.

MWM X X

Diagram 4.11k: Conflict between the slim Wood element and the big semicircle representing Metal.

FFFF X

Diagram 4. 11l: This logo is divided into four sections. An indication of disintegration. This is inauspicious.

MF X X

Diagram 4.11m: Inauspicious — Metal is in conflict with Fire.

FM X X

Diagram 4.11n: This logo is completely disintegrated. Most inauspicious logo for a company.

FFFF ✓✓

Diagram 4.11o: This logo is divided into four sections representing four partners, but the sections are united in the middle. A good logo that shows ideal integration and harmony for staff and partners. If the cross-shaped connection in the center were missing, the logo would have a negative effect (compare with Diagram 4.11l).

CHAPTER 5
Landscape and Space Affect Business Performance

The influence of mountainous landscape

Over the years I have traveled widely, visiting hundreds of communities in many different parts of the world. The landscape varied from flat, open terrain to very steep rugged mountain ranges. While visiting these communities I observed people's behavior and general way of life. I noticed, for example, that communities in very steep mountainous areas all had a distinctive pattern of very restrictive behavior. The more enclosed the mountain ranges, the more closed and restrictive were the minds and the behavior of the people who lived there (see Diagram 5.1). As a result of their environmental conditions, these communities have had to be more self-reliant and therefore tend to have a superior attitude that makes it difficult for them to accept another person's point of view. Many Swiss, Northern Italian and Austrian people living in the European Alps have these closed-minded characteristics.

These enclosed communities tend to perceive more obstacles and problems in their daily life and in their aspirations. Why?

Every day, when these people open their doors, they see in front of them high mountains that are then translated subconsciously as obstacles in their daily life. While totally enclosed mountainous regions are a very restrictive influence on all who live there, some mountain ranges are less invasive than others. Two parallel ranges of mountains still exert some restrictive influences, however they are an improvement (see Diagram 5.2).

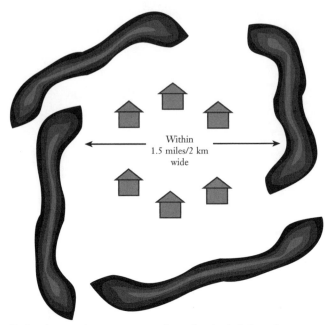

Diagram 5.1: Enclosed mountain ranges create unique, closed-minded people.

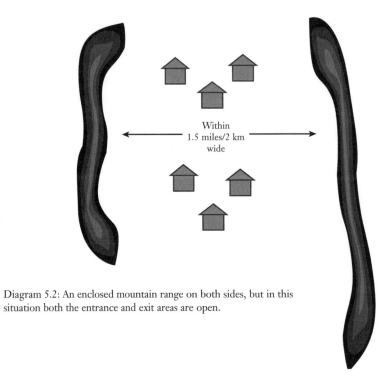

Diagram 5.2: An enclosed mountain range on both sides, but in this situation both the entrance and exit areas are open.

The communities in Diagram 5.2 would be less restricted than those in Diagram 5.1. The narrow-mindedness of the people changes when the distance between the ranges is increased (see Diagram 5.3). There is more freedom of movement and communities travel more widely.

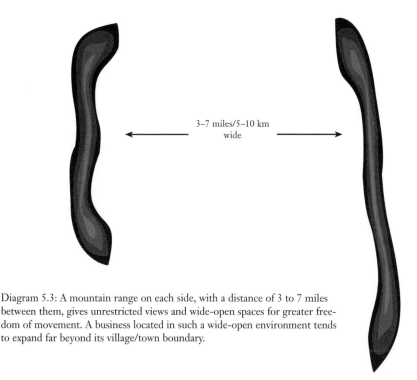

3–7 miles/5–10 km
wide

Diagram 5.3: A mountain range on each side, with a distance of 3 to 7 miles between them, gives unrestricted views and wide-open spaces for greater freedom of movement. A business located in such a wide-open environment tends to expand far beyond its village/town boundary.

Inner and outer business landscape

Ever heard the saying, "What you see is what you get"? What we see or what we think about most of the time, in terms of images and pictures, is what we will manifest as a reality in our lives. As we notice it daily it makes an impression on our minds, even if an unconscious one. Its influence will be felt in every aspect of our lives, in our personal relationships and in our business.

The way we perceive our environment and our life in general and the conclusions we draw — often unconsciously — creates a certain "inner landscape" which is also manifested outside. From this, a visible and perceptible "corporate landscape" evolves, which is reflected in our business in the following ways:

> *In a retail business, it will be reflected in the way we display our goods, our attitude towards customers, and our general demeanor when we are dealing with the public.*
> *In an office it will be evident in the way we arrange our fixtures and furniture, the way we do our business, and our general behavior and attitude towards clients.*
> *Overall its influence will affect our goals and vision for the future.*

The objects and features that are in our environment affect the way we think and feel; they influence our attitudes towards people, the way we want our business done, and our aspirations for our own lives and for society. All these influences can be either positive or negative and, as a result, either attract or push customers away.

The conditions we create around us become the cultural and behavioral pattern that then affects the cosmic life force. When the cosmic life force is thus programmed, it affects the people as they work in their office or business premises. This pattern of behavior is often called the "corporate culture." It needs a strong chief executive to change some aspects of this environmental culture.

If we want to change our business psychology and attitudes, we need to change the pattern of influence that has been impressed on the cosmic life force around our business. This can be achieved by making the following changes:

> *Make Feng Shui changes to the overall layout and arrangement of fixtures and furniture to improve energy, harmony and oxygen levels.*
> *Start renovations that include a change of color scheme, and use designs in furniture and fixtures that are in harmony with the business and clientele.*
> *Change our personal attitude and behavior. Be more willing to take an open-minded approach, and be more receptive to new ideas and modern technology.*
> *Employ a new manager/boss to introduce more substantial changes quickly. Experience has shown that businesses usually do well in the first six to twelve months after a new manager takes over. A better result is often achieved with major changes. Of course, positive changes are more effective in sustaining long-term profitability and success.*

The internal business landscape

The business landscape inside a building affects a person's frame of mind and overall attitude to work. According to Feng Shui, walls can be compared with mountains. Many partitioned offices in large business premises create many "internal mountains" (see Diagrams 5.4a–c). The major difference between a natural mountain and an office wall is that the enclosed office is more rigid and inflexible in actions, movements and communications, thereby creating many more obstacles than a natural rolling mountain range. Enclosed offices tend to establish an "isolated empire" for individuals who then feel cut off from their colleagues. Granted, enclosed offices have their merits. They give privacy, and promote a quieter atmosphere with fewer disturbances. But too many completely enclosed offices (mountains) in business premises are detrimental to smooth-flowing communication, a sense of comradeship and effective teamwork (see Diagrams 5.4b–g for more illustrations).

Diagram 5.4a: The shape of a natural mountain.

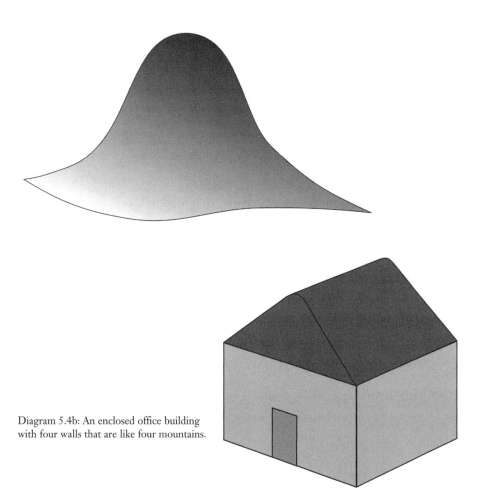

Diagram 5.4b: An enclosed office building with four walls that are like four mountains.

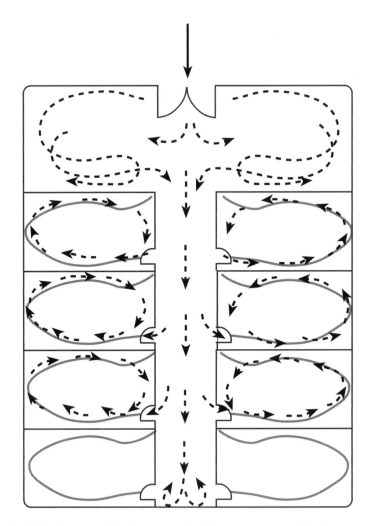

Diagram 5.4c: Eight "mountains" have been created in this business premises, blocking energy and communication flow. Unnecessary obstacles have been created to make this a situation unsuitable for a business in today's economy.

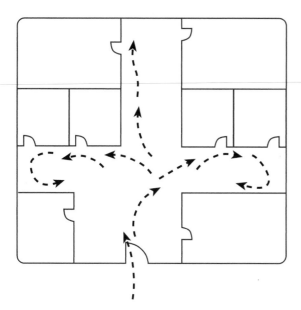

Diagram 5.4d: Restricted movements in the flow of energy. It would be very difficult to create a good working team.

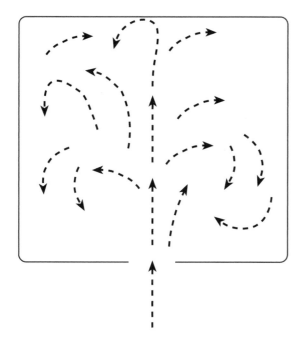

Diagram 5.4e: The energy flow and movements are unrestricted in this room where there are no partitioned offices.

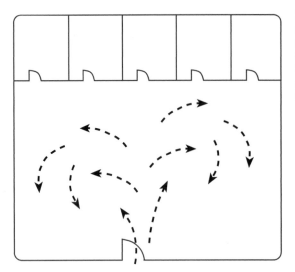

Diagram 5.4f: This partially enclosed office floor plan facilitates easier communication between staff who are more friendly to each other and to their customers. The energy for a good working team is generated automatically.

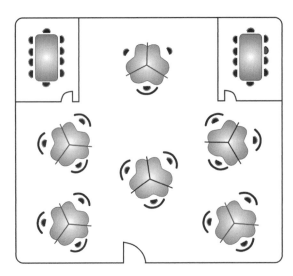

Diagram 5.4g: This is a possible arrangement that would generate good energy flow and freer communication between the staff members.

In an open-plan office, staff members tend to be more relaxed in expressing themselves and are more likely to create a better working team because they have the opportunity to communicate easily. With fewer walls there is a greater flow of cosmic life force and energy throughout the large room. Workers also tend to be more active and have higher vitality.

Workers in Diagram 5.4d would tend to be restrictive in their movements and communication. When workers are enclosed in cubicles they tend to be more political, and more defensive of their "enclosed empire" or "fortress." Some workers actually seek those enclosed spaces because of their own lack of confidence.

From many years of experience in giving consultations on office layouts, I find it exceptionally difficult to create a successful working environment for a business in these enclosed and blocked-off environments. For any business to be successful, especially in the very challenging twenty-first century, office layouts will need to be arranged to suit a flexible work team. The new economy requires high-tech rapid communication, which depends on quick responses and high-speed changes to make the most of all business opportunities.

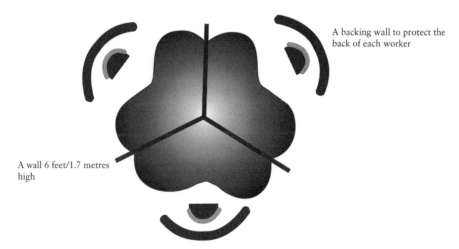

A backing wall to protect the back of each worker

A wall 6 feet/1.7 metres high

Diagram 5.4h: The tripartition office layout.

The tripartition office layout

A triple-partitioned area allows free flow of cosmic life force and oxygen. It gives more freedom of movement to workers who can move around freely and communicate with their colleagues. In the twenty-first century success in business will depend on good communication with a fast flow of information. This open design provides these requirements.

The main purpose of business is to communicate our ideas, products and services to our customers. How can we communicate to people outside our business, when we cannot communicate to colleagues within our working team who are restricted by unnecessary walls (mountains)? Furthermore, when business executives sit facing a wall, they tend to be less creative and successful. They also tend to be self-centered and unable to work effectively in a team. An open-plan office arrangement is the more acceptable standard in office layout for modern office life.

Smaller mountains in small offices

The next situation to consider is the space within individual offices. The open space of an office is like an open landscape that is completely clear of any obstacles like trees, small hills, rocks, and so on. Every piece of furniture we put into an office creates obstacles (mountains) to block or direct the flow of cosmic life force energy and oxygen and any beneficial energy movements. Not all "mountains" in an office are negative; it depends on where we place them. The basic rule is: it is generally good Feng Shui to have "mountains" behind where we sit to give us strong support and backing (see Diagram 5.5a). "Mountains" in front of us are considered to be obstacles. Therefore as far as possible we should avoid placing tall furniture or fixtures in front of, or near, our desk (see Diagram 5.6).

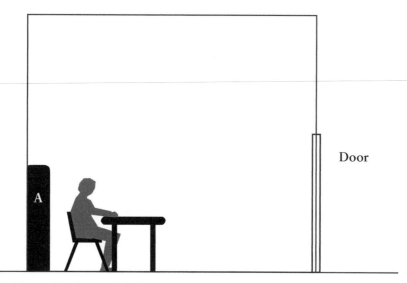

Diagram 5.5a: A low cupboard (A) at the back gives excellent support and backing for the person working in this room. In Feng Shui interpretation, the backing enhances this person's success in work and therefore he/she will receive more support from subordinates and colleagues.

Diagram 5.5b: The high cupboard (B) is overwhelming the person and therefore suppressing his/her ability to work more effectively. The cupboard creates suppressive energy and causes unnecessary pressure over the head and body of the person sitting in the chair. This type of situation appears to give a good backing, but on the contrary becomes a large burden that impedes effective work performance.

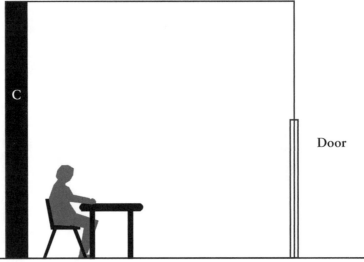

Diagram 5.5c: The tall floor-to-ceiling cupboard is like a wall. However, it does not constitute a threat unless the cupboard has no doors and the books and shelves are exposed. Then it is negative, for the open shelves generate plenty of turbulent energy and cause aggressive movements of energy in the room.

Diagram 5.6: Cupboard A obstructs the person's view and creates an energy in the room that would prevent the person working here from enjoying free expression and a sense of moving forward in life. The cupboard is like a tall mountain causing indecisiveness and an inability to be proactive and positive. This person would generally lack any vision for the future.

CHAPTER 6
A Strong Backing is the Key to Business Success

To define a "strong backing" I liken it to a person sitting on a chair. If a chair has a strong back support then we feel comfortable to sit on it knowing we will not fall down. Good backing (for example, a hill or a solid wall) in Feng Shui is generally interpreted to mean that we receive strong support from our family, our friends, customers, mentors, bankers and government.

Backing is classified into five categories with each one just as essential as the other in contributing to a successful business. Most important is the backing of:

> *The commercial building*
> *The main corporate office*
> *The floor where the chief executive's office is situated*
> *The offices of the chief executive and financial controller*
> *The chief executive's and controller's seating locations.*

Backing for commercial buildings

A commercial building is like a person. When we sit in our workplace we need to sit on a solid, strongly built chair with good support behind us so that we can keep our balance and concentrate on doing our work with the minimum of stress. A commercial building must be built on a solid base with a strong, solid backing that gives protection and comfort in all working areas where employees are seated. However, the backing should not be more than one third of the height of a building, otherwise it would have an overwhelming effect (see Diagrams 6.1a–b).

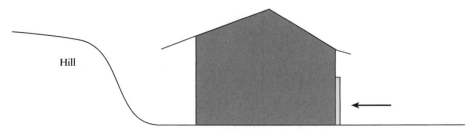

Diagram 6.1a: A hill to the rear provides good backing for the building.

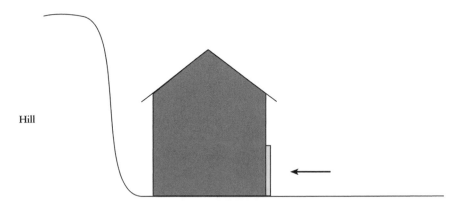

Diagram 6.1b: The hill behind the building gives backing but is too high and overwhelms. It is therefore inauspicious.

The buildings in Diagrams 6.1c–f are examples of a bad backing and urgently need substantial Feng Shui remedies to avoid further business failures.

A "well-seated" building is one that has a good backing with the correct height. It is interpreted to indicate that the company has a strong base from which to grow and move forward. The staff members feel more secure and in balance.

The buildings in Diagrams 6.1c–f are not solidly seated. While working in these buildings the occupants would tend to have a feeling of insecurity and generally feel unsafe. This atmosphere would generate endless problems in work and in decision making. Staff would have a high incidence of depression and anxiety.

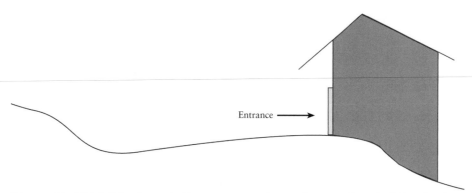

Diagram 6.1c: This building has no backing or support to the rear. Occupants have the feeling that the building is falling backwards and would therefore tend to have back problems. A business situated in such a building is usually less successful.

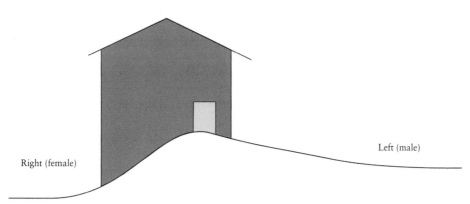

Diagram 6.1d: This building is unstable and is "sliding" towards the right (female) side. Women working in this building would be less successful and unable to keep their jobs.

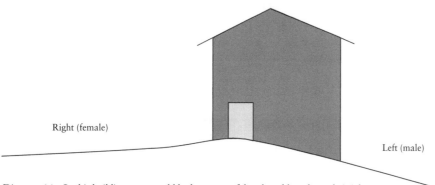

Diagram 6.1e: In this building men would be less successful and unable to keep their jobs.

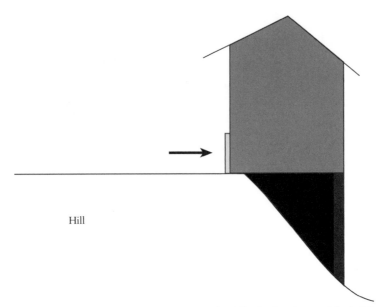

Hill

Diagram 6.1f: This building looks as if it is clinging to the cliff. The foundation of the building is very weak for business stability. It is a most inauspicious commercial building with a business failure rate of over 80 per cent within three to five years for any type of business.

How to check the energetic stability of a building

You can try a simple experiment to confirm whether a building is stable in terms of energy. As you stand inside such a building facing the main entrance door, close your eyes. Place your palms on both sides of your thighs. Now feel for yourself in which direction the building's energy is moving. If you are in a building that has been built on a slope, you will experience a sensation that it is falling towards the sloping sides. I have found that more than 80 per cent of participants at my courses were able to sense the imbalance of buildings that were built on slopes.

In this context it is important to emphasize that we do not refer to the architectural stability of the building but to the energy flow inside and outside the house.

As the building in Diagram 6.1a has such a stable foundation, you do not feel or perceive any movement in this building. In Diagram 6.1c the back of building is on a down slope. You will have a feeling of falling backwards, as if the building is going to slide down the hill. In such a building most occupants, especially the executive staff, would be inclined to suffer from balance problems, severe back problems, and other associated health difficulties.

The feeling in the building in Diagram 6.1d is slightly different. The building is "moving" towards the right (or female) side. Females working in such a building would tend to lose control over their performance and be less successful. The health of the occupants would be affected in varying ways depending on where they sit. If they were sitting facing the main entrance then they would have a feeling that they were falling towards their right side. They would therefore put more pressure on their right limbs to prevent themselves from falling. Over time they would tend to develop stress on the right side of the body. Prolonged periods of sitting in this location could cause circulation problems, spinal curvature, and numbness in the right limbs. If they were sitting with their backs towards the sloping side, they would experience a sensation of falling backwards, and suffer regular back problems and severe back pain. I found many business premises of this type where 80 per cent of the occupants had some kind of spinal problem.

Those occupying the building in Diagram 6.1e would experience the opposite effects from those in the building in Diagram 6.1d. However, since the left (or male) side is sloping, male occupants in the building in Diagram 6.1e would tend to be more negatively affected than females. The building in Diagram 6.1f is an extreme case of a very inauspicious commercial building. The whole building would appear to be falling backwards. It would not matter how strongly the building was reinforced to avoid a physical slide. Occupants in this building would tend to lack confidence and often develop a phantom fear that would weaken their kidneys. In these circumstances it is very likely that they would be unable to concentrate or make any intuitive decisions. I seldom see successful businesses in this type of building.

How can this situation be remedied?

In Feng Shui practice an experienced consultant would be able to apply heavy concrete blocks, metaphysical remedies and symbols to neutralize the sensation of movement and lack of backing in these buildings.

In one instance in Switzerland, a situation similar to that in Diagram 6.1f was remedied at a cost of less than US$1000. Depending on the location, it is also possible in some cases to change the entrance to another side to create an improved backing. Often this remedy involves additional construction work and higher cost. An unsuccessful and struggling business often turns around quickly once it has been stabilized. Owners of businesses occupying buildings similar to those in Diagrams 6.1c–f should engage an experienced Feng Shui consultant to remedy the defect before profits suffer.

The backing inside the building

A building must have an outside backing — for example, a hill or another building — as well as a solid wall at the back of the office, which serves as the backing inside. The following examples show how the backing can be affected by glass walls, missing areas and windows.

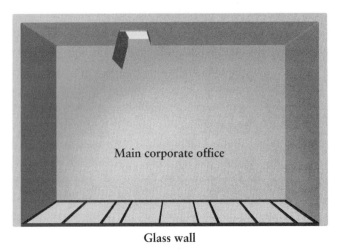

Main corporate office

Glass wall

Diagram 6.2a: Inauspicious. This corporate office has a glass wall at the back. It indicates that its backing is fragile like the glass, and success is uncertain.

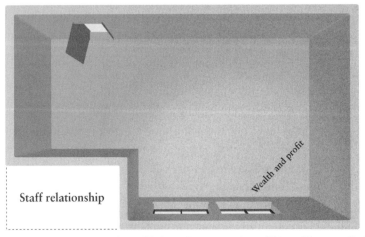

Staff relationship

Wealth and profit

Diagram 6.2b: A major back section in the Staff Relationship area is missing. This could cause staff relationship problems apart from an imbalance in the backing. This building is not suitable for a major corporate office.

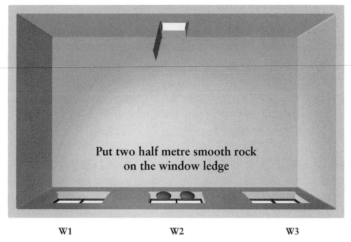

Put two half metre smooth rock on the window ledge

W1   W2   W3

Diagram 6.2c: The middle "spine" of a building is best left with a solid wall to give the office a good backing. In this example there is a window (W2) in the middle of this corporate office where the "spine" is located that is weakening its good backing. This can be remedied by placing two to three smooth rocks (about 24 inches/50 centimetres high) on the window ledge. These rocks create a symbolic mountain to enhance the backing for this office. Better still, seal the W2 window completely.

The backing of the office rooms

The floor occupied by the chief executive of a company also requires a strong backing to give the chief executive the strong support of his or her corporate team who work on this particular floor.

The chief executive and financial controller or treasurer are the two most important positions in an operating company. Their offices must have a strong backing to give them a solid base.

Remedies to strengthen the backing

The absence of a strong, solid backing at the end of the offices of the chief executive and financial controller/treasurer can be corrected by putting up a solid divider or bushy plants. Alternatively, where there are large windows or a glass wall to their back, these can be sealed off using special opaque foil or opaque glass blocks to give the solid backing that is required.

Case study

I remember the case of a company in Germany. The chief executive was sharing the same floor as the five vice-presidents. He was continually handicapped because they did not support him on major policy issues. The back of the main corporate office was made of glass. The chief executive was sitting with his back towards a section of the glass wall. I suggested they place a row of solid dividers ($8^1/_4$ feet wide by $6^1/_2$ feet high or 2.5 metres by 2 metres) along the full length of the glass wall. Although my suggestion may have sounded silly and impractical — the dividers blocked some natural light and some of the good window views — the remedies were urgently needed. On my insistence the solid dividers were built in, more for the experiment than a belief that it would change things positively for the chief executive of the company. Three months after the placing of the solid wooden dividers, I received a thank-you card from the chief executive saying that he generally felt a strong shift of consciousness in the corporate office. His vice-presidents were now more receptive to his ideas and vision than before.

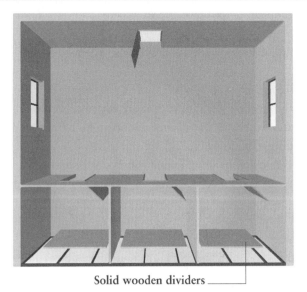

Solid wooden dividers

Diagram 6.3: Solid wooden dividers (8¼ feet wide by 6½ feet high or 2.5 metres by 2 metres) to give a strong backing to the main corporate office and individual senior executive offices.

A strong backing for the chief executive's seating location

The chief executive or manager running a company must sit in a location where he/she has a solid wall at his/her back. A solid wall provides the strong support that would be expected from subordinates.

However, readers are reminded that sitting in a strong command location in an office is more important, for we can always use remedies to create a solid backing for the office (see Diagram 6.4).

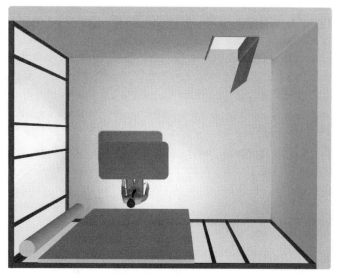

Diagram 6.4: This chief executive has a good view and command of the company. A solid divider provides a strong backing to give protection where he/she sits.

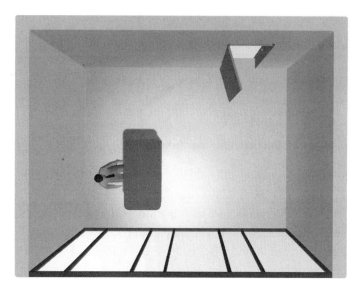

Diagram 6.5: This chief executive does not have effective control of his/her company. Even though he/she has a solid backing, the door opening is placed on the wrong side.

Remedy — change the door opening to the opposite side so that the manager can see more clearly as people come into the office.

Glass-walled buildings — a modern catastrophe

From research carried out in the USA, Australia, Hong Kong, Thailand and Europe, companies occupying glass-walled buildings have a higher incidence of failure.

Although it is a modern trend to build glass-walled commercial buildings for business transparency, in fact it is not good Feng Shui. A glass wall gives a sense of insecurity; it is less stable than a wall and can break more easily. Glass walls leak much cosmic life force energy and oxygen from a building. Furthermore, everything can be observed through the glass. There is a higher chance that the company's secrets will be passed on to someone outside.

On the other hand, a company that can comply with all the above-mentioned categories of a strong backing is usually a strong, successful company.

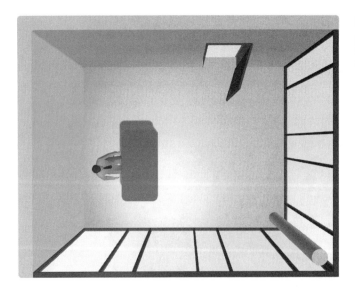

Diagram 6.6: This is a good seating position for a chief executive or manager of a company.

A strong backing for the main corporate office

In a situation where a main corporate office is occupying one floor in a high-rise building, the main corporate office must also have a strong backing to its rear. A strong backing symbolically indicates that the corporate powerhouse of the company is solidly based, has a good, strong foundation, and has the support of the board, bankers, shareholders and customers.

CHAPTER 7
Who Is the Boss?

Chief executives or managers are responsible for the management and profitability of their company. However, whether they have effective control in their role does not depend solely on higher academic qualifications or practical knowledge and experience but where they sit in the office and where in the building their office is located. The boss should sit in the so-called "command position," which will be explained in this chapter. Most businesspeople are unaware of this important factor.

I have often found that the offices of highly effective managers who maintain the profitability of a company are found in the command position of a company.

The office of chief executives or managers determines in a sense their spiritual and psychic command. If their office position does not give them complete command of the company, they will not have the full backing of the staff. The full support of subordinates in a company is imperative to create a productive team.

I have seen a chief executive of a large German corporation with gross profits of several billion who was unable to command the respect of his vice-presidents. A brief ten-minute assessment on where to locate his seating position gave him one hundred per cent effective control and turned around his company.

The command room position in an office floor plan
As a Feng Shui rule, the room diagonally farthest away from the main entrance is the

most supportive room for the top executives; let us call it the "command room." Furthermore, the office is assessed according to the Eight Life Aspirations, the door opening, the exact position of the desk, and so on.

The Diagrams 7.1–8 show different types of office arrangements with command rooms in different locations.

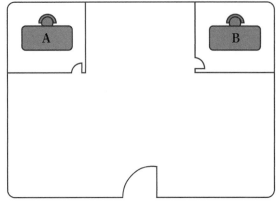

Diagram 7.1: Room A is the command room position. You can see that the opening of the door of room A and the main door are diagonally opposite. Room A receives more cosmic Qi and oxygen than B. According to the Eight Life Situations it is also in the Prosperity and Wealth area of this floor plan. A senior person should sit in room A.

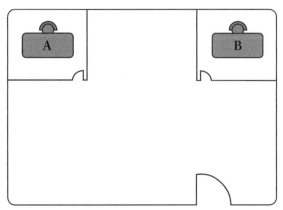

Diagram 7.2: Room B is the command room position because the occupant receives more cosmic Qi and is able to clearly see people coming into the office.

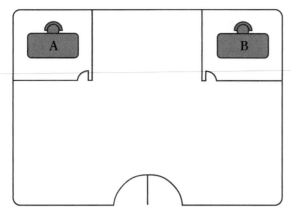

Diagram 7.3: Here the main door is open on both sides. The chief executive or a senior manager of a company should sit in room A, the Prosperity and Wealth area of the office plan of the whole building. The chief needs to ensure good profit for the company.

Room B is in the Relationship area in the office floor plan. The personnel or staff relations executive should sit in room B to guide and control good relationships within the company. If the chief executive is sitting in room B, then the company may have good staff relationships and possibly a good relationship with clients, but may be less profitable because too much of the chief's time is spent in public relations work.

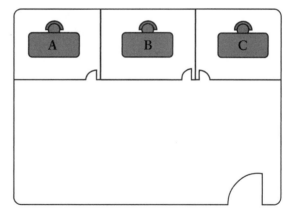

Diagram 7.4: The best command room position is A followed by B and then C. Generally, the room that is diagonally furthest away from the main entrance door is the most powerful leadership room. Room A is the best room for a chief whose priority for the company is making a good profit. If the chief occupies room B, the company would be well known but may not be very profitable, as room B is in the Fame area of the office floor plan. Room B would be suitable for a senior government official to occupy.

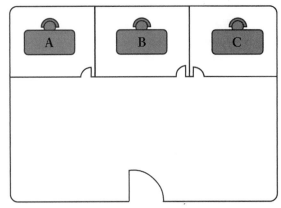

Diagram 7.5: Room C is the best command position as the occupant has the best command view of the entrance door. Although Room A is also in a good command position, the door opening position reduces the quantity of good Qi from entering the room from the main door. Without a sufficient quantity of benevolent Qi going into Room A, the occupant would not be able to perform well or make sound, intuitively based decisions.

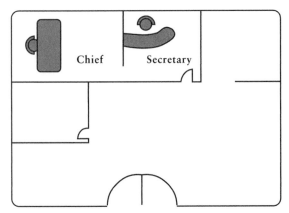

Diagram 7.6: In this example, the secretary who is sitting in the Fame area is actually running the company. On many occasions I have observed this situation.

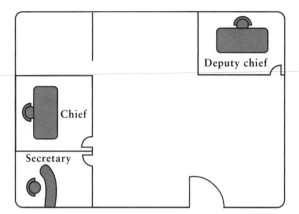

Diagram 7.7: The deputy chief is effectively running the company. The chief's room is too close to the main door where there is too much disturbance and is in the Family area. This influence would make him/her show more interest in family and family relationships than in having effective control and management of the company.

Diagram 7.8: If the chief executive occupies a lower floor than his/her immediate senior subordinate, it makes him/her subservient to them. This position makes him/her unable to take full command or receive the respect necessary to effectively manage the company. The chief executive would be unable to receive the full cooperation of subordinates.

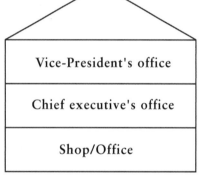

Case study

A chief executive of a $150 million corporation often had problems getting respect or majority agreement for his strategic business plan from his six vice-presidents. The chief executive was a very capable and effective person. His plans had proved to be sound and successful, yet often he had to spend a lot of time explaining his proposals and then specifically directing several of his vice-presidents to carry out these plans.

A Feng Shui study was carried out to assess whether the problems between the chief executive and his vice-presidents were caused by personal difficulties or by other factors. It was identified that the main cause of disrespect for the chief executive was a Feng Shui problem. Diagram 7.9a shows the location of the chief executive's office and his seating position. Note that the chief executive's room is not in the command position in the company. Secondly, it is located too close to the entrance and is there-

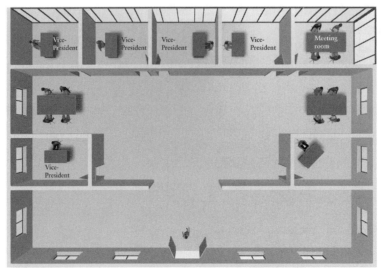

Chief Execuitve
Officer

Diagram 7.9a: The former office of the chief executive.

fore open to continual distraction. His desk was placed where he could sit facing a view of the sea, as he liked to observe the movement of ships and boats coming into the bay; however, he had no control over the company.

Remedies for the chief executive's office

Ideally, the best position for the chief executive was the room in the right corner occupied by one of his vice-presidents. The chief executive's room was therefore moved to area B of the building (see Diagram 7.9b). Area B represents the Relationship area that will improve the relationship between him and the vice-presidents. A solid divider was placed immediately behind the chief executive's back to give him solid support and to block the draining of his energy out through the glass wall. A robust "money plant" (*Portulacaria afra*) was placed in corner B to enhance prosperity and also improve relationships with staff.

A bushy plant was placed in the corner marked C to stop the auspicious Qi energy and oxygen that was coming in through the office door from bouncing out through the glass wall opposite. A fountain in the center of the office floor is pulling in more Qi energy; the solid divider placed in the E area diverts Qi energy into the vice-presidents' offices. The boardroom is now placed in the most auspicious command position at A, so that the chief executive can make the best decisions.

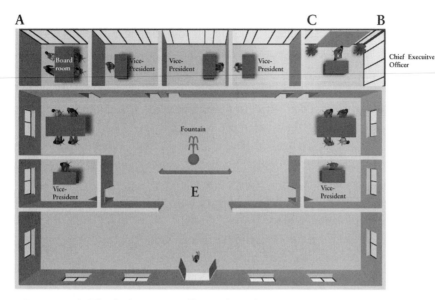

Diagram 7.9b: The chief executive's office is relocated to area B.

After the Feng Shui remedies were implemented, the chief executive was readily accepted as the chief of the company and received the full cooperation and support of his vice-presidents and board members. As a further result of the Feng Shui remedies the company's profitability improved by more than 50 per cent in two years.

Selecting the right sitting position for negotiations and talks
According to the principles of Feng Shui, you can select an auspicious sitting position and then be able to sell something to somebody even though the product you have for sale is not wanted urgently. In such a location you can also use this technique to sell ideas and projects to your superior or subordinates to obtain full cooperation in implementing projects.

Over the last thirty years it has been the Chinese, Japanese and South Koreans who have most often been able to obtain better terms in trade negotiations with Americans and Europeans, just by knowing intuitively where the most powerful positions are in a meeting or conference room. In a meeting room or a conference hall there is always one most powerful and commanding location in which to sit or stand to ensure that you have a better command. I call this the "commander-in-chief position."

Even if very junior members of a negotiating team sit in this position, they will receive respect for every word they say. If, as a senior member of a negotiating team, you are sitting in the command position at a meeting and you talk less and listen more attentively, usually you are able to influence the outcome with your insights or ideas and receive the most benefits from the meeting.

How to determine the command position of the speaker or chairperson

Very often we give credit for a successful meeting to the skill of the chairperson, but seldom do people ask why the chairperson was so effective. I have attended meetings chaired by the same person but in different meeting rooms. Not all the meetings ran smoothly, even with the same group of people. In some more difficult and seemingly impossible meetings to chair, a chairperson managed to get through smoothly with excellent results. On the other hand, some meetings with a seemingly straightforward agenda presented many obstacles.

Thirty years ago, when I noticed this phenomenon for the first time, it puzzled me and I asked myself why it occurred. I had a great desire to one day become chief executive of a large company, where I would have to chair meetings. I knew from my observations that when a chairperson is effective, they usually get more business done and in doing so often gain the respect of their team and colleagues.

As I became more involved in Feng Shui, I discovered many phenomena that affect the performance of chairpersons and presenters. As I continued to observe, two important factors that affected the performance of a speaker or chairperson became very clear to me: Normally, about 70 per cent of the success of a meeting depends on the chairperson's mastery of meeting procedures and personal charisma. The other 30 per cent is determined by the internal seating arrangements of a meeting room and where the entrance door is placed in relation to the position of the chairperson. This little-known psychic command position determines a chairperson's ability to command the attention of the audience or participants at a meeting.

At a meeting, the person in the command position is like an army officer of the highest rank, commanding a respect that considerably influences the outcome of that meeting. There are many important rules to guide a person who wants to locate the command position and the five other advantage positions in a meeting room. Here are a few guidelines:

> The seating position in the room that is farthest from the main entrance door, and from which you are the first one able to see a person coming into a room, is the command position. The head of the table should also be located in this position.

> At the back of this command position there should be a solid wall for a good backing.

> *From this position you should be able to see the door of the office room.*
> *Ideally, from this position you are also facing the main entrance to the office, even though you may not be able to see the main door because there are walls in between.*

The following diagrams show the best control positions. You may not be lucky enough to find such an ideal position unless you are the chief or the chairperson of the meeting. However, there are more auspicious sitting positions, which will be explained in the diagrams below.

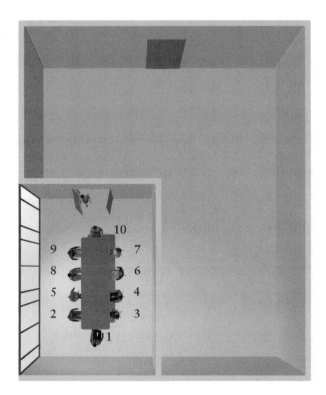

Diagram 7.10: Number 1 indicates the most influential and powerful position to sit in a meeting. Number 10 is the most inauspicious position with the back facing the door.

Energy flow

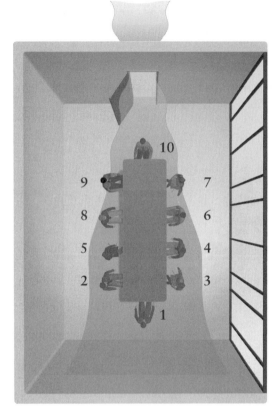

Diagram 7.11: Even though the number 1 position at the head of the table is the command position, it is weakened by the direct yet subtle "attack" of energy from the main door.

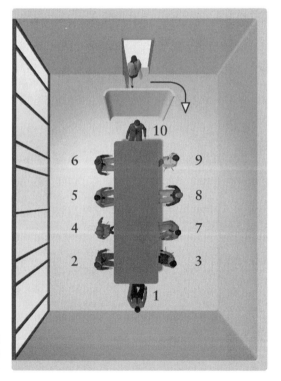

Diagram 7.12: Remedy for Diagram 7.11: Install a divider/screen between the door and the conference table.

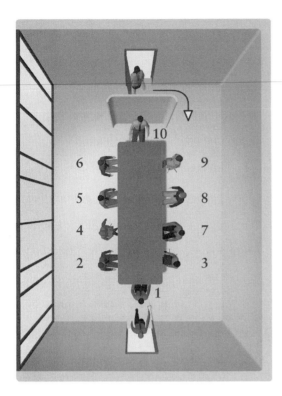

Diagram 7.13: The number 1 position is weakened with the door at the back. This situation is most common in hotel conference rooms. If the chairperson occupied this position, he/she would not be very effective in controlling the meeting.

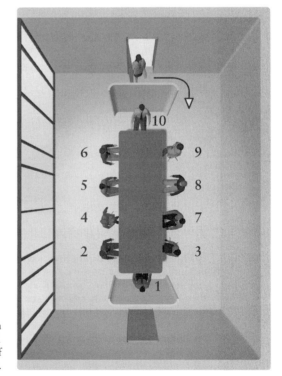

Diagram 7.14: Remedy for Diagram 7.13 — install a solid wooden divider at the back of the number 1 position. The back door is locked for the duration of the meeting so that nobody can open the door.

Auspicious and inauspicious seating positions

Several examples are shown to assist a group in the selection of the best seating positions.

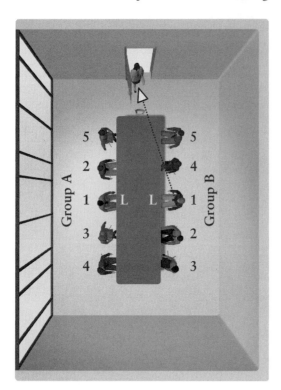

Diagram 7.15: When both groups are sitting opposite each other with the leader (L) in the middle, the best command positions are on the right side of the meeting hall where group B can easily see those coming into the room. The door opening on the right side also gives group B more of the vitalized Qi energy and oxygen. The best seating positions are numbered from 1 to 5, with number 1 being the best and number 5 the least advantageous of all.

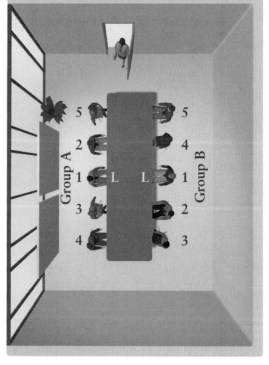

Diagram 7.16: Although group A is supposedly occupying the best seating positions, they are sitting with their backs towards the window, giving them a weak backing position even if curtains are available. In this situation, those in group B are sitting in better positions and are able to receive good support and have an edge over group A. Numbers 1 to 5 indicate preferred seating positions. Remedy: Place dividers or plants at the back of the members of group A.

In summary, the most effective position for a person chairing a meeting to command respect and authoritative power is where he/she has the first view of all the persons coming into the room. This position must also have a solid wall behind or a solid divider will need to be installed to give this position protection and a feeling of security and stability that instills confidence. In this position the chairperson is in complete control of the meeting and the meeting space, and is effectively yet impartially able to conduct the proceedings of the meeting. Furthermore, it makes sense if the entrance to the meeting room is at the back, so that the audience is not disturbed when people come into or leave the meeting; they can pay full attention to the chairperson or speaker.

Layout of meeting and lecture rooms

The twenty-first century is an era of competition. Up-to-date information, knowledge and business skills are very important to improve productivity and enhance business success. It is necessary for business executives to be informed continually of new developments and innovations by attending seminars and workshops.

Over the last five years I have given sixty to eighty lectures each year in fifteen countries. I have found that seventy to eighty per cent of conference and meeting rooms have been badly designed and are not really suitable for the purpose intended. Most often the seating arrangements are so bad that the speakers or chairpersons do not have effective control of the meeting to capture the attention of the audience. With the incorrect placing of the entrance door, an audience is constantly distracted by people who come into the conference or meeting at random intervals.

Two years ago I was asked to select some good seminar halls in Europe with a capacity for 150 to 300 participants. I looked at eighty facilities in Germany, Switzerland and Austria, but only found three that were suitable.

Hotels and conference organizations should be more sensitive to the requirements of speakers. Tremendous opportunities exist in North America and Europe for investment in meeting and conference facilities designed according to Feng Shui principles.

The following illustrations show some positive and negative examples of meeting and lecture rooms.

Diagram 7.17: Auspicious arrangement for speakers. The group will be more attentive and retain more information from the speakers because they sit with their backs facing the door.

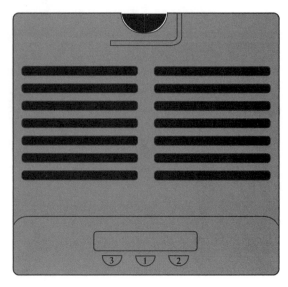

Speakers

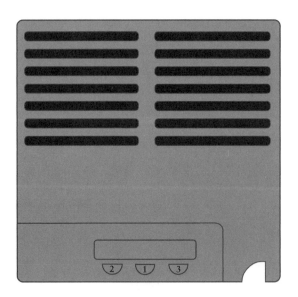

Speakers

Diagram 7.18: An inauspicious room arrangement. In this meeting hall it would be the audience "controlling" the chairperson or speaker who gets tired very easily. The audience can see the door and would be constantly disturbed as people come in and out of the hall. It is very difficult to get issues discussed and resolved, and people are more irritated.

Diagram 7.19: An inauspicious arrangement for the entrance door. This hall is not suitable for a conference. In fact, the speaker only controls the half of the audience who cannot see the door. There is too much distraction from the door, as half of the audience can see people coming and going.

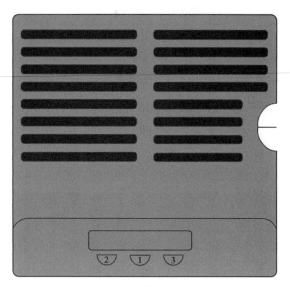

Speakers

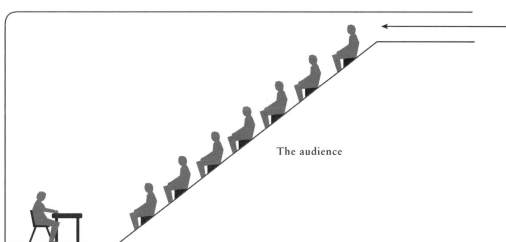

The audience

Chairperson/speaker

Diagram 7.20: An inauspicious arrangement. This type of arrangement where students or an audience look down on the speaker is not suitable for delivering a good lecture. An overpowering audience would dominate the discussion and results would be biased. Many university lecture halls are arranged in such a way. Students sitting in a tiered seating arrangement that dominates the professor would be inclined to express themselves more freely while the professor would have a less prominent role.

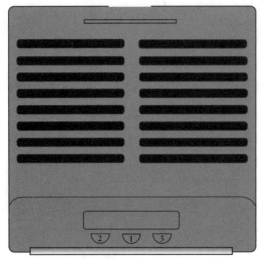

Glass wall

Diagram 7.21: An inauspicious design for a conference hall.

In Diagram 7.21, although the chairperson, speaker or lecturer appears to have the full attention of the audience, in reality the control is ineffective. The glass wall at the back causes an outward pull of energy thereby weakening his/her position. This situation is similar to that of a person sitting on a chair with a weak backrest and wobbly legs. A person lacking a solid backing would tend to suffer from a lack of confidence.

The standard remedy for Diagram 7.21 is to place a solid divider at least six feet/two metres wide between the window and the speaker's chair. Lecturers giving frequent seminars of several hours in this type of hall would be totally drained and would generally need to expend more effort to convince the audience. Many experienced lecturers teaching in a hall like this have often complained to me that the audience drained their energy.

CHAPTER 8
Feng Shui Rules for Career Success

Your potential for career advancement may be enhanced by several basic Feng Shui factors. As described in the previous chapters, you should have a solid backing, the right command position, and avoid facing the "Grand Duke Jupiter," as well as have auspicious directions for your sitting position and office.

The size of your office

Where a person sits in an office is not usually considered very important. More often, the emphasis is on having a huge office to give the impression of being important. The bigger the office is, the bigger the ego and the power and authority that comes with it. This is the physical power game in the workplace. The more important psychic and spiritual aspects are seldom understood or considered.

Actually, the size of an office does not give a person any real power or control over the work, the working team or their performance. The real and often overwhelming, but subtle, control comes from where a person sits in a room and his or her harmony with this place.

An ambitious and progressive person occupying an office should sit in the command position so that physically, emotionally and psychically the person is in full control. Occupying this position, one is more relaxed, less stressed, has better concentration, and is able to make more rational yet intuitively based decisions. Promotion prospects are then enhanced many times.

If you want to further enhance your performance and success, you should observe the following rules — according to priority and as explained by diagrams:

1. *You have to sit in the "command position."*

2. *When looking straight you must not face the direction where "Grand Duke Jupiter" is located.*

3. *You must have a solid wall at the back.*

4. *Your workplace should be in a good compass direction according to the East–West System, and at the same time you should face an auspicious direction. The room door should face one of your best directions.*

Rule 1: You must sit in the commanding position.
The diagrams below show several auspicious sitting positions.

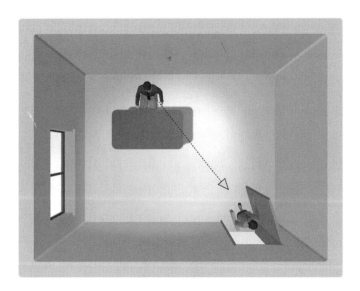

Diagram 8.1: A good seating position. Occupant sits diagonally opposite the door to have a clear view of the door and have a solid wall at his/her back.

Inauspicious sitting positions to avoid:
> *Do not sit with your back facing the door.*
> *Do not sit directly in the "door line."*
> *Avoid a sitting position immediately next to the window.*

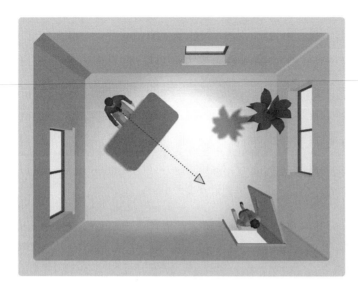

Diagram 8.2: A good seating position, provided that the corner of the room at the back of the person is rounded off as indicated. If the corner at the back is not rounded off, then the energy moving towards the corner creates a suction effect, pulling the person backwards and causing a balance problem.

Diagram 8.3: A good seating position provided that the table is at least three feet from the window.

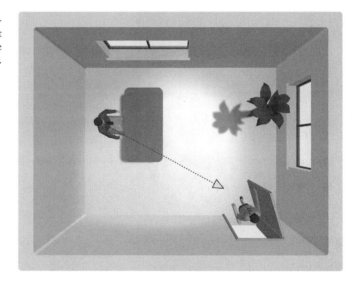

Sharing office space

When two or more persons share an office it is important to select a good seating position to enhance promotion prospects.

Rule 2: You must not face "Grand Duke Jupiter."

According to ancient Chinese Imperial Palace protocol, to avoid disasters and problems in administration it was decreed that senior officials should not sit facing the planet Jupiter. Jupiter was given the name "Grand Duke" in accordance with the need to give due respect.

As Jupiter moves in its orbit around the sun, its location changes each year to a different compass direction attributed to the astrological animal symbol of the current year. For example, in 1996, the year of the Rat, the Grand Duke's position was in the north. In the year 2001, the year of the Snake, Jupiter's position was in the south-south-east.

Due to the strong magnetic beam of the planet Jupiter, it is not advisable to sit in an office facing the Grand Duke. From experiments carried out, I have found that people who sit directly facing the direction of Jupiter may feel a loss of balance, become more easily tired and make more mistakes. You can, however, sit with your back to the Grand Duke.

It is highly recommended that you avoid carrying out any renovations, construction or earth works if the work is taking place in the direction of the Grand Duke. For example, in the year 2001 when the Grand Duke was in the south-south-east direction, no renovations or alterations should have been made in that sector of a room,

Table 4: Compass Directions for the Planet Jupiter (the "Grand Duke")

Year	Astrological Animal Sign	Compass Direction
1995	Pig	NNW
1996	Rat	N
1997	Ox	NNE
1998	Tiger	ENE
1999	Hare	E
2000	Dragon	ESE
2001	Snake	SSE
2002	Horse	S
2003	Sheep	SSW
2004	Monkey	WSW
2005	Rooster	W
2006	Dog	WNW
2007	Pig	NNW
2008	Rat	N
2009	Ox	NNE
2010	Tiger	ENE
2011	Hare	E
2012	Dragon	ESE
2013	Snake	SSE
2014	Horse	S
2015	Sheep	SSW
2016	Monkey	WSW
2017	Rooster	W
2018	Dog	WNW
2019	Pig	NNW
2020	Rat	N

office or building. See Table 4 for the compass directions of the planet Jupiter for the next two decades.

Rule No. 3: You must have a solid wall behind your back.
This point has already been discussed in chapter 6.

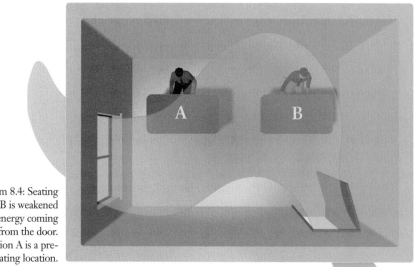

Diagram 8.4: Seating position B is weakened by the energy coming in from the door. Position A is a preferred seating location.

Energy flow

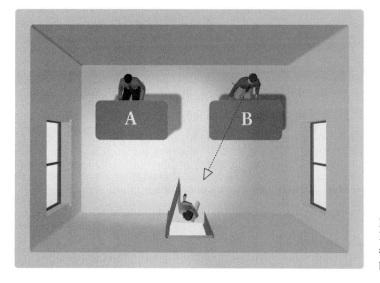

Diagram 8.5: Position B is the area to sit for fast promotion.

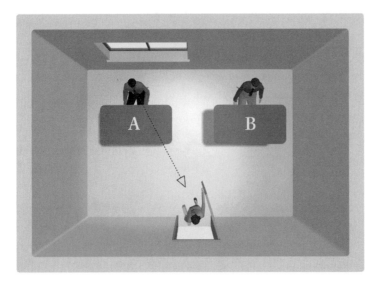

Diagram 8.6: Position A is not a preferred position because the window at the back undermines the strong backing. The preferred seating position is B. Although promotion may be a little slower, it will come.

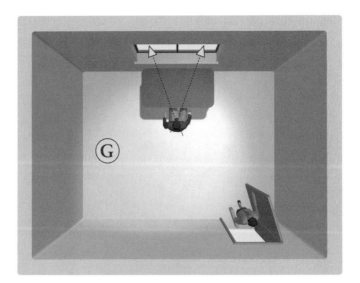

Diagram 8.7: This is the most inauspicious place to sit in an office. Many office workers prefer sitting here. They would have no control over their work and destiny, would be inclined to withdraw and therefore not be a good team member. Persons sitting with their back towards the door are often found to be nervous and tend to make mistakes. The outside views would be a constant distraction that reduces concentration and effectiveness. In a competitive environment this person's chances of getting quick promotion are low. Remedy — move to sit in the area marked G with the back facing the wall, looking towards the door.

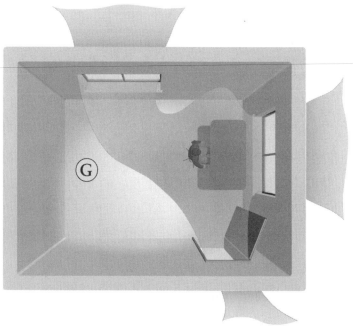

Energy flow

Diagram 8.8: This seating position is slightly better than the one in Diagram 8.7, because the person can see the door. However, there is a negative health effect. Office workers sitting along the path of the door entrance receive the direct "attack" of the energy coming into the room. Occupants would tend to suffer from nervousness and heart problems if sitting in this position for more than three years.

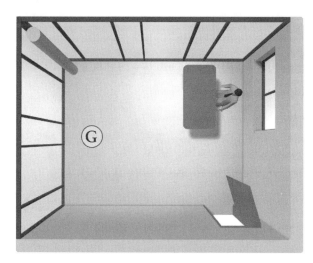

Diagram 8.9: This office worker is sitting in a really inauspicious position in direct line with the door, with his back towards a window and the side next to a glass wall less than one yard/one metre away. This person would probably suffer from heart problems and "height syndrome disease," nervousness and tremors in the hands, if sitting in this position for more than three years. If all windows were from floor level to ceiling height, then the symptoms would develop faster. Remedy — move to sit in the position marked G and place a full-height cupboard or a divider behind the chair.

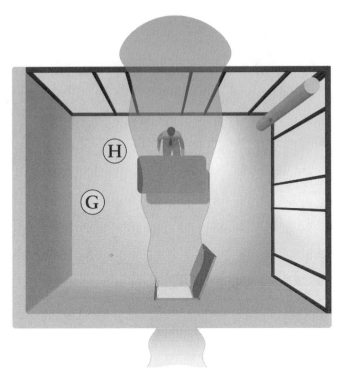

Energy flow

Diagram 8.10: This seating position may appear to look very good, but in reality it is not so. The flow of cosmic energy coming into the room is strongly directed at the person, giving him/her a "push" out towards the glass wall. Since the cosmic energy and oxygen easily permeate the glass wall, together they cause an outward suction effect. After several weeks of sitting in this position, the person would tend to suffer from heart problems, in particular if the office is located on the upper floors. This person would have a balance problem and be unable to concentrate. More mistakes would be made in decisions and performance would generally be below expectation. Remedy — move to sit in the position marked G, or move to sit in position marked H but put a solid, full-height cupboard behind the chair. In position G the person should sit with the back facing the wall.

Rule No. 4: Use your most auspicious compass direction.

Your workplace should be located in an auspicious compass direction, while at the same time you should face one of your auspicious directions. The door of the room should also be located in one of your four best compass directions.

Apart from the command position and the Grand Duke Jupiter, the auspicious personal compass directions are a vital factor. They are determined according to the East–West System (see chapter 8). This system was developed by the ancient Taoist masters and is based on their observations and astrological building calculations.

NW	N (A3)	NE
W	Centre	E (A1)
SW	S (A2)	SE (AA)

Diagram 8.11: The four most auspicious compass directions for a female with the Personal Trigram K'AN are marked in gray on the floor plan of her office. She can now place her chair in one of these four auspicious directions.

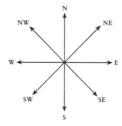

Depending on the direction a building is facing, different types of Qi are entering the building to spread in certain areas.

By using your birth year you can now determine the group you belong to and find your auspicious compass directions. These are the areas suitable for your workplace in the office.

How do you apply the best compass directions principle when you place your chair and table in your office? An example will show you how to determine the position of your desk according to your most auspicious compass directions. In chapter 9 you will find more detailed information on how to find your personal compass directions and identify auspicious areas within the building.

Let us take a simplified example of a woman born in 1950 with the Personal Life Trigram K'AN (water). The best compass directions for K'AN are in the following order: 1) south-east, 2) east, 3) south, and 4) north. Therefore she should sit in her office in the south-east sector which is marked AA in Diagram 8.11.

In Diagram 8.12, this woman is sitting in the south-east which is her best compass direction area in the room, with her back towards a solid wall. She is sitting facing north, her fourth best direction, and can also see the door clearly. The door is also

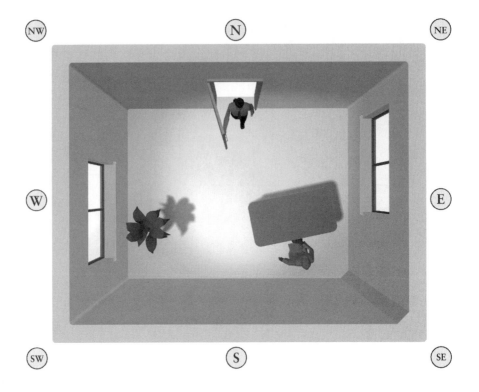

Diagram 8.12: Very auspicious seating position for a woman born in 1950.

open in her auspicious direction — south-east. This seating position could be called the "Golden Jackpot" position. Her prosperity and respect from her colleagues will be further enhanced when sitting in the "Prosperity" area according to the Eight Aspirations system. A robust money plant (Portulacaria afra) is placed in the room to filter the air from toxins.

CHAPTER 9
Auspicious Spaces in the Office According to the East–West System

A key factor in Business Feng Shui is the selection of the most auspicious "power place" to sit and work. This space, which is individually matched, will enhance your health and personal peak performance. I will explain in simple terms how you can find the most auspicious spaces and rooms to occupy in a building so that you can work in harmony, maintain high vitality and therefore achieve more.

The Eight Trigrams East–West Group Building System (in short the Eight Buildings System), also known as *Ba-Tza* or *Eight Residences*, is based on the ancient Chinese Imperial Palace system of construction. In ancient times, palaces were built according to the compass directions and seasons so that the emperor and his family could live in different auspicious palaces throughout the year. In Diagram 9.1 you see the Chinese compass face, the *Lo'pan*, which is still used today to determine the various sectors. In this diagram the Lo'pan is divided into eight sectors of 45° degrees each. Each sector is considered a separate direction in Feng Shui.

An auspicious area is selected in the following manner:

› *The Trigram of the building and the location of the auspicious and inauspicious areas are identified.*
› *The Personal Life Trigram of the respective person as well as his/her auspicious directions are determined.*

> *The auspicious areas of the building and the person as well as his/her elements are matched.*

> *After selecting the most auspicious office room the exact position of the workplace is determined.*

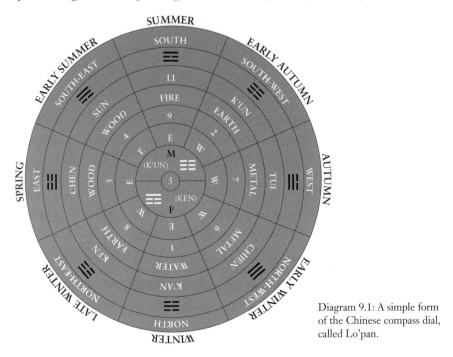

Diagram 9.1: A simple form of the Chinese compass dial, called Lo'pan.

Determining a Building's Trigram

In order to find auspicious locations in your building, you begin by determining which Trigram (in Chinese *Kua*) your building belongs to. Just follow these steps to find the building Trigram for a specific building.

Find the "sitting position" of the building

A building's Trigram is determined by its "sitting position" — that is, the direction where the back of a building is located. Normally the front of the building is opposite the back of the building.

Diagrams 9.2a–e show that although all the doors are placed at different locations along the front of the building, this does not alter the fact that the sitting positions of the building are in the south.

Facing North

Diagram 9.2a: The entrance is in the middle.

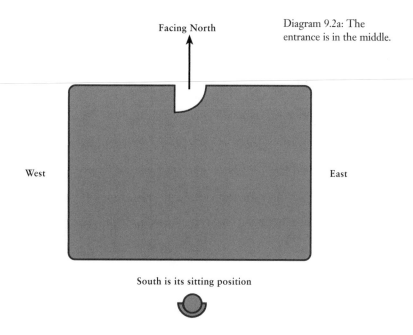

West

East

South is its sitting position

Diagram 9.2b: The entrance is at the front left.

Facing North

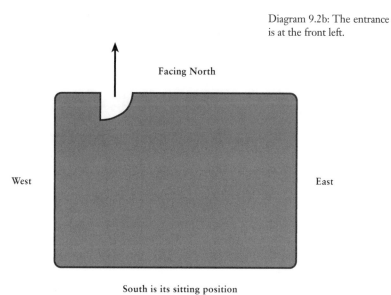

West

East

South is its sitting position

Diagram 9.2c: The entrance is at the front right.

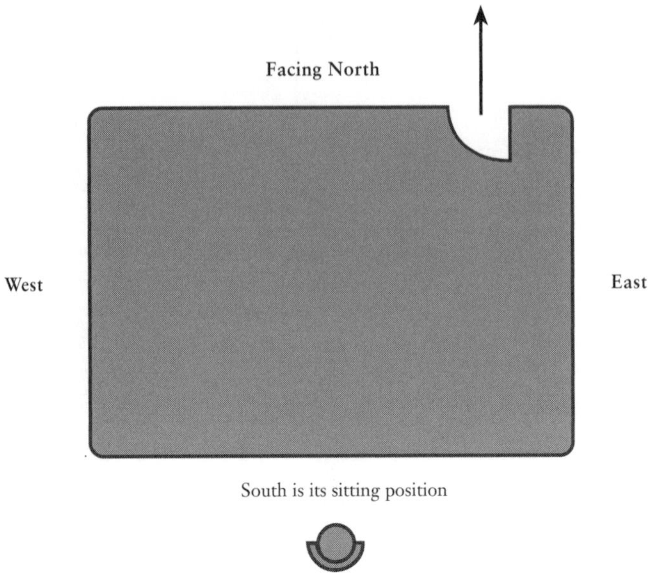

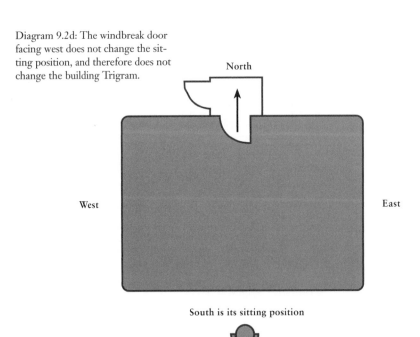

Facing North

West

East

South is its sitting position

Diagram 9.2d: The windbreak door facing west does not change the sitting position, and therefore does not change the building Trigram.

North

West

East

South is its sitting position

Diagram 9.2e: The windbreak door
is facing north-west. The main door
is actually facing north. The sitting
position is still south.

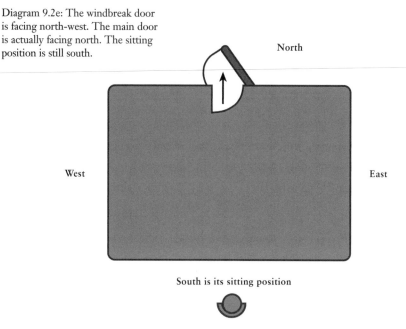

North

West

East

South is its sitting position

Determine the direction of the sitting position of the building

On the assumption that the front and back of a building are parallel, we can also determine the sitting position of the building at the front of the building.

Usually the House Trigram is determined by a compass reading in front of the door. To take a reading you may take a Lo'pan or an ordinary compass and place the compass against the door from outside. It is more accurate to take two to three readings at different distances from the door. Next you step one yard/metre away from the door, and then ten feet or three metres away, and take the second and third readings.

To get an accurate reading, there should be no reinforced concrete and no objects made from magnetic metal (iron, steel, cobalt) nearby. All three readings should be the same. Different readings may be caused by metallic contents of the door or steel reinforcing under the floor. In this case a fourth reading about seventeen feet or five metres away from the door has to be taken.

For modern buildings, the third and fourth compass readings should be the same and normally more accurate than the first two. Alternatively, two compass readings can be taken from the center of the back wall and another reading ten feet (three metres) away. When the front door and back wall readings vary substantially, the back wall readings are often found to be more reliable. Readings that differ considerably from the other readings do not count.

Remember that compass readings will differ if metal stairs, handrail, grille, or a parked car is within five feet (1.5 metres) of your compass. Your heavy metallic watch and big belt buckle may also affect your compass readings. Avoid reading a compass indoors in a modern building with a reinforced concrete floor unless you use a calibrated ship's compass. Your reading will not be accurate. The reading may also be affected by electrical wires inside or outside the wall.

Determine the Trigram and its direction

For example, your reading is 5° north at the door — the facing side of the building. The back of the building, which is opposite the front, is 185° south — the sitting position of the building. As the sitting position determines the Trigram, the building in our example belongs to the LI Trigram.

Now look at the Chinese compass dial in Diagram 9.3d with the Trigram LI (Fire element) in the middle. You can see that there are four auspicious compass directions on the dial (marked as A-areas) and four inauspicious compass directions (marked as D-areas). These subdivisions are also seen on the other compass dials.

East Group Building Trigrams

Auspicious (A) and inauspicious locations (D)

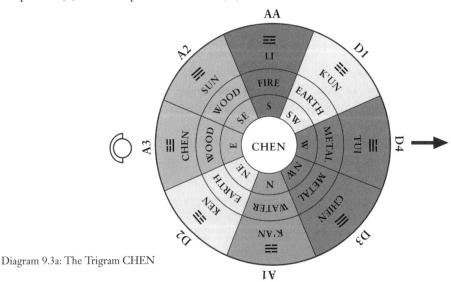

Diagram 9.3a: The Trigram CHEN

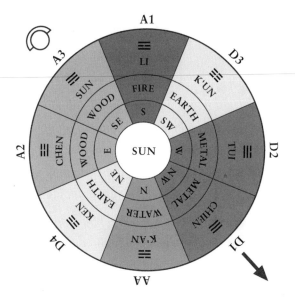

Diagram 9.3b: The Trigram SUN

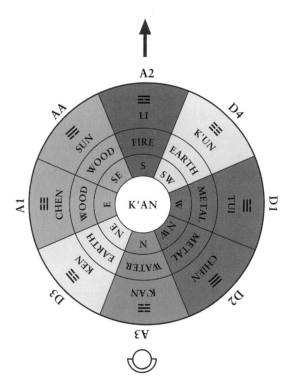

Diagram 9.3c: The Trigram K'AN

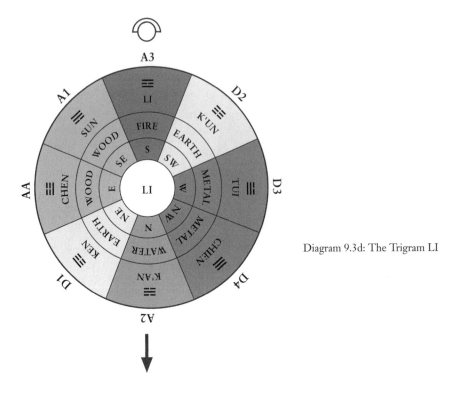

Diagram 9.3d: The Trigram LI

West Group Building Trigrams

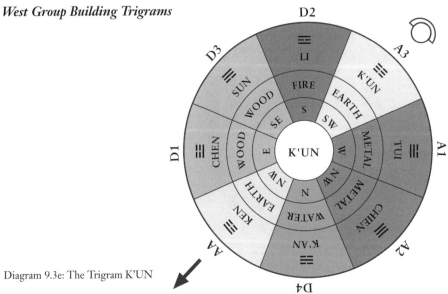

Diagram 9.3e: The Trigram K'UN

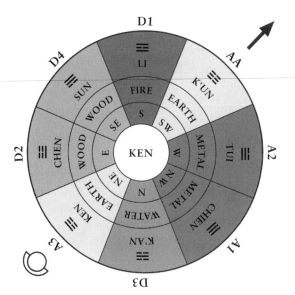

Diagram 9.3f: The Trigram KEN

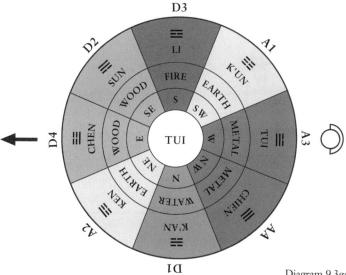

Diagram 9.3g: The Trigram TUI

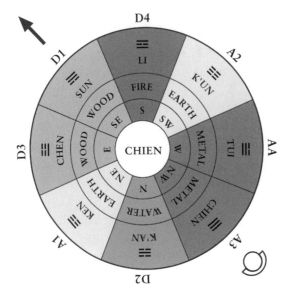

Diagram 9.3h: The Trigram CHIEN

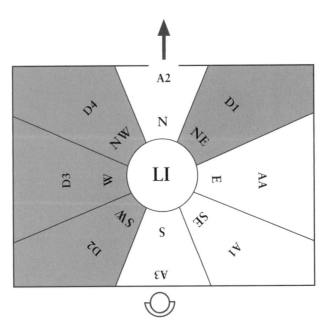

Diagram 9.4: This is a LI Trigram building with the respective ratings.
The sitting of the LI building is at the south and the facing is north.

The basic rule is that the entrance and the most frequently used rooms should be located in A-areas. Rooms in D-areas should be less frequently used, for example as warehouse, storage and washrooms.

Let us continue with our example: The compass dial with the ratings for the LI Trigram is now placed on the building plan (see Diagram 9.4). The areas marked with the letter A are the four auspicious locations while the areas marked with the letter D are the inauspicious. The most auspicious location for a LI building Trigram is AA — in the east.

The door is in area A2 which is auspicious. It would be auspicious to place important offices in the east (AA), south-east (A1) and south (A3) areas. The best places for

Grading	Point score	Chinese term	Interpretation and effects
Table 5: Interpretations for Auspicious Locations			
AA	+80	SHENG QI	*Sheng Qi* means highly vitalized energy. Good to locate main door, working table and seating area here. Enhances good intuition and success in career. *High achievement and good fortune.*
A1	+70	TIEN YI	Tien Yi literally means *Doctor from Heaven*. This area gives healing, love and caring Qi. It enhances good health, healing and safety. *Success, good health, abundance, reliable employees and friends.*
A2	+60	YIEN NIEN	*Yien Nien* implies extending time, longevity and posterity. Good for relationships, manager potential and career. *Good income and harmony, at work and with family.*
A3	+55	FU WEI	*Fu Wei* refers to self-improvement. This location enhances personal abilities and capacities for growth in career and finance. *Good management of personal affairs.*

the store, the toilet, or less important offices are in the D areas, especially D4 which should be used for the store or toilet.

For a more detailed interpretation you will find key words for the A and D areas in the Tables 5 and 6.

Grading	Point score	Chinese term	Interpretation and effects
		Table 6: Interpretations for Inauspicious Locations	
D1	-60	WHO HAI	*Who Hai* implies more prone to accidents and mishaps. For this location occupants are likely to incur small accidents, small lawsuits and problems at work. *Disharmony, small problems and potential legal problems.*
D2	-70	LIU SHAH	*Liu Shah* means *Six Sufferings.* Occupants in this area may encounter arguments, divorces, legal problems, unprofitable business. *Prone to accidents, unsuccessful career, bad influences and money problems.*
D3	-85	WU KUEI	*Wu Kuei* means *Five Ghosts.* This area may attract unwanted spirits/ghosts or negative energy causing disharmony, frequent quarrels, fire and burglary. *Some small misfortunes and loss of money.*
D4	-90	CHUEH MINGH	*Chueh Mingh* means *Total Loss* or life-threatening danger. Loss of property, degenerative diseases, bankruptcy, bad luck for male children and general bad luck. *Lack of wealth, loss of job and severe health problems.*

In Feng Shui practice we determine the auspicious locations so that we can utilize the space to our advantage. The A-areas maintain our balance and harmony in general. Sitting in a room with a Trigram rating of AA would enhance intuition and good decision making. Inauspicious areas should otherwise be avoided. The working principle is: use the spaces marked A more often and the spaces marked D less often or avoid them completely. If you do not have a choice, use the D-area as little as possible.

Look at the area where the front door is located

It is always preferable to open a business door in an auspicious compass direction with beneficial cosmic life force energy and oxygen coming in through the A-areas. The energy of the A-areas would benefit the business by enhancing staff performance and attracting more customers. Exceptions are the Trigrams CHEN and CHIEN which do not have auspicious A-areas in the front.

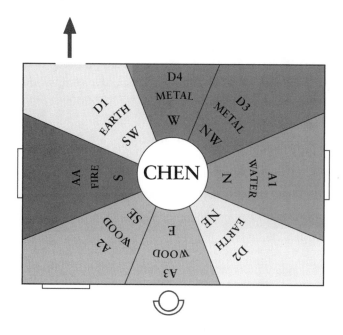

Diagram 9.5: The CHEN Trigram does not have an A rating for an auspicious front door opening.

In such a situation, you have different possibilities:

> *You can open a door in the less negative south-west (D1) sector. The south-west direction is attributed to the Earth element which is more negative due to the energy of the D-area. By*

using specific Feng Shui measurements the Earth element energy and thus the influence of the D-area is reduced. According to the principle of the Five Elements (see chapter 3), we apply the "child" of Earth which is Metal (Metal is draining Earth). In this case we can place a large metal figurine or a metallic object near the door to reduce the negative Earth energy and stabilize the D1-area. If you do not have any other choice because the front door is located in a more inauspicious D-area, you follow the same principle — weaken the element of the direction where the D-area is located by using the element of the "child."

› *Alternatively, or in conjunction, you can also open a side door at the south (AA) or at the north (A1) to tap more Qi energy flowing through an A-area. In this case you use the south-west (D1) door less often and try to come into the office from the south or north doors.*

› *If you cannot open a side door at the south or north area, then you should try to build in a window in these directions and open it often to bring more vitalized beneficial Qi energy into the building. You can also open the windows at the south-east (A2) sector more often.*

Remember that you have to continue to use the inauspicious south-west (D1) door. If you are exclusively using the south (AA) or north (A1) doors as front doors, the Building Trigram would have to be determined again and this would change to KAN or LI respectively, then new area gradings according to the respective compass dial (see Diagram 9.3a–h).

How to determine the Personal Life Trigram for individuals

Not only each building has a Trigram but the individual as well. The Personal Life Trigram and the respective element is determined by the birth year. According to the A- and D-gradings for the directions, we identify the areas which are auspicious for a certain individual. There is an interaction between human and building depending on their directions.

The Personal Life Trigram, which you can determine by using Table 7, is calculated according to the lunar calendar. The years with an asterisk start from February 4; years without asterisk start from February 5.

Example: The year 1968 began on February 5. If you were born between February 5, 1968 and February 3, 1969, your Trigram is K'UN (Earth) if you are a male. If you are a female, your trigram is K'AN (Water).

Please note: If you were born before February 5 in 1968, your Trigram year is 1967. If you are a male, your Personal Life Trigram is CHIEN (Metal), and if you are female it is Li (Fire).

Table 7: Birth Year, Personal Life Trigram and Personal Trigram Element

Abbreviations: W = Water, WD = Wood, F = Fire, E = Earth, M = Metal. (* years start on February 4)

Year	Trigram Male	Trigram Female	Year	Trigram Male	Trigram Female
1900*	K'AN (W)	KEN (E)	1930*	TUI (M)	KEN (E)
1901*	LI (F)	CHIEN (M)	1931	CHIEN (M)	LI (F)
1902	KEN (E)	TUI (M)	1932	K'UN (E)	K'AN (W)
1903	TUI (M)	KEN (E)	1933*	SUN (WD)	K'UN (E)
1904	CHIEN (M)	LI (F)	1934	CHEN (WD)	CHEN (WD)
1905*	K'UN (E)	K'AN (W)	1935	K'UN (E)	SUN (WD)
1906	SUN (WD)	K'UN (E)	1936	K'AN (W)	KEN (E)
1907	CHEN (WD)	CHEN (WD)	1937*	LI (F)	CHIEN (M)
1908	K'UN (E)	SUN (WD)	1938*	KEN (E)	TUI (M)
1909*	K'AN (W)	KEN (E)	1939	TUI (M)	KEN (E)
1910	LI (F)	CHIEN (M)	1940	CHIEN (M)	LI (F)
1911	KEN (E)	TUI (M)	1941*	K'UN (E)	K'AN (W)
1912	TUI (M)	KEN (E)	1942*	SUN (WD)	K'UN (E)
1913*	CHIEN (M)	LI (F)	1943	CHEN (WD)	CHEN (WD)
1914	K'UN (E)	K'AN (W)	1944	K'UN (E)	SUN (WD)
1915	SUN (WD)	K'UN (E)	1945*	K'AN (W)	KEN (E)
1916	CHEN (WD)	CHEN (WD)	1946*	LI (F)	CHIEN (M)
1917*	K'UN (E)	SUN (WD)	1947	KEN (E)	TUI (M)
1918*	K'AN (W)	KEN (E)	1948	TUI (M)	KEN (E)
1919	LI (F)	CHIEN (M)	1949*	CHIEN (M)	LI (F)
1920	KEN (E)	TUI (M)	1950*	K'UN (E)	K'AN (W)
1921*	TUI (M)	KEN (E)	1951*	SUN (WD)	K'UN (E)
1922*	CHIEN (M)	LI (F)	1952	CHEN (WD)	CHEN (WD)
1923	K'UN (E)	K'AN (W)	1953*	K'UN (E)	SUN (WD)
1924	SUN (WD)	K'UN (E)	1954*	K'AN (W)	KEN (E)
1925*	CHEN (WD)	CHEN (WD)	1955*	LI (F)	CHIEN (M)
1926*	K'UN (E)	SUN (WD)	1956	KEN (E)	TUI (M)
1927	K'AN (W)	KEN (E)	1957*	TUI (M)	KEN (E)
1928	LI (F)	CHIEN (M)	1958*	CHIEN (M)	LI (F)
1929*	KEN (E)	TUI (M)	1959*	K'UN (E)	K'AN (W)

1960	SUN (WD)	K'UN (E)	1990	K'AN (W)	KEN (E)
1961*	CHEN (WD)	CHEN (WD)	1991	LI (F)	CHIEN (M)
1962	K'UN (E)	SUN (WD)	1992	KEN (E)	TUI (M)
1963*	K'AN (W)	KEN (E)	1993	TUI (M)	KEN (E)
1964	LI (F)	CHIEN (M)	1994	CHIEN (M)	LI (F)
1965*	KEN (E)	TUI (M)	1995	K'UN (E)	K'AN (W)
1966*	TUI (M)	KEN (E)	1996	SUN (WD)	K'UN (E)
1967*	CHIEN (M)	LI (F)	1997	CHEN (WD)	CHEN (WD)
1968	K'UN (E)	K'AN (W)	1998	K'UN (E)	SUN (WD)
1969*	SUN (WD)	K'UN (E)	1999	K'AN (W)	KEN (E)
1970*	CHEN (WD)	CHEN (WD)	2000	LI (F)	CHIEN (M)
1971*	K'UN (E)	SUN (WD)	2001	KEN (E)	TUI (M)
1972	K'AN (W)	KEN (E)	2002	TUI (M)	KEN (E)
1973*	LI (F)	CHIEN (M)	2003	CHIEN (M)	LI (F)
1974*	KEN (E)	TUI (M)	2004	K'UN (E)	K'AN (W)
1975*	TUI (M)	KEN (E)	2005	SUN (WD)	K'UN (E)
1976	CHIEN (M)	LI (F)	2006	CHEN (WD)	CHEN (WD)
1977*	K'UN (E)	K'AN (W)	2007	K'UN (E)	SUN (WD)
1978*	SUN (WD)	K'UN (E)	2008	K'AN (W)	KEN (E)
1979*	CHEN (WD)	CHEN (WD)	2009	LI (F)	CHIEN (M)
1980	K'UN (E)	SUN (WD)	2010	KEN (E)	TUI (M)
1981*	K'AN (W)	KEN (E)	2011	TUI (M)	KEN (E)
1982*	LI (F)	CHIEN (M)	2012	CHIEN (M)	LI (F)
1983*	KEN (E)	TUI (M)	2013	K'UN (E)	K'AN (W)
1984*	TUI (M)	KEN (E)	2014	SUN (WD)	K'UN (E)
1985*	CHIEN (M)	LI (F)	2015	CHEN (WD)	CHEN (WD)
1986*	K'UN (E)	K'AN (W)	2016	K'UN (E)	SUN (WD)
1987*	SUN (WD)	K'UN (E)	2017	K'AN (W)	KEN (E)
1988*	CHEN (WD)	CHEN (WD)	2018	LI (F)	CHIEN (M)
1989*	K'UN (E)	SUN (WD)	2019	KEN (E)	TUI (M)

Table 8: Dividing the Trigrams into East and West Groups

The East Group

Trigram	Direction	Element	Compatible with
K'AN	North	Water	Metal, Water
CHEN	East	Wood	Water, Wood
SUN	South-east	Wood	Water, Wood
LI	South	Fire	Wood, Fire

The West Group

Trigram	Direction	Element	Compatible with
K'UN	South-west	Earth	Fire, Earth
KEN	North-east	Earth	Fire, Earth
CHIEN	North-west	Metal	Earth, Metal
TUI	West	Metal	Earth, Metal

As we have seen from the compass dials (Diagrams 10.3a–h), the Trigrams and their elements can be divided into two groups — East and West. This principle applies to the Personal Life Trigram as well as the House Trigram (see Table 8). In the most auspicious case a person and a building belong to the same group, as they have the A- and D-ratings in common. If a person and a building belong to different groups, the A-areas of the person are located in the D-areas of the building and vice versa.

How to match the areas for building and individual

To determine which is the most auspicious room in an office for an individual to occupy and to enhance a person's intuition, performance and good promotion prospects, we have to consider three main factors:

> The office should be located in one of the A-areas of the Building Trigram.
> The best compass direction sectors (A-areas) should be in accord with the Life Trigram of the person.
> The individual's Personal Life Trigram element (see Table 7) should be in harmony with the element of the building's location.

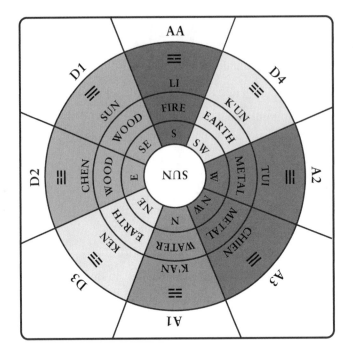

Diagram 9.6: The area ratings for the Personal Life Trigram SUN.

As an example, we have a male office worker, Mr. Y, born on August 16, 1960. He will move into an office in a LI building. We have already determined the A-areas of the LI building by using the compass dial (Diagram 9.3d). Now we want to find Mr. Y's Personal Trigram.

We look at Table 7 — "Personal Life Trigram and Personal Trigram Element" — under 1960 for males. Mr. Y's Personal Life Trigram is SUN, Wood element. (A female born in the same year would have the Personal Life Trigram K'UN with the Earth element).

Next we look at the compass dial in Diagram 9.3b with SUN 4 in the center to find Mr. Y's auspicious (A) and inauspicious (D) areas in the office.

For the SUN Trigram, the best compass direction is north (AA). The next best directions are south (A1), east (A2) and south-east (A3). Mr. Y's worst direction, or direction to avoid, is north-east (D4).

Now these Personal Life Trigram ratings are translated into an office situation. In the diagram below we compare the ratings of Mr. Y's Personal Life Trigram SUN and the Building Trigram LI.

In general terms the east with AA (A2), south-east with A1 (A3) and south with A3 (A1) are the most auspicious locations for Mr. Y to use as his office. However, we should also consider Mr. Y's Trigram element which is SUN — Wood. If he should decide to occupy the south (Fire element), he would need to use an earth-colored carpet as an additional remedy. According to the mother-child rule (see chapter 3), he would weaken the Fire with Earth. Another choice would be a natural-colored wooden floor (wood supports Wood), or a small water fountain near his working table (water strengthens Wood element).

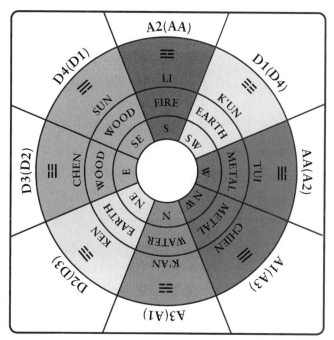

Diagram 9.7: The LI Trigram of the building is combined with the SUN Trigram of Mr. Y. The directions' ratings for his Personal Life Trigram are put in brackets.

Point scoring system for area assessment

In the beginning it is often difficult to determine the best area of a building or room as different influences have to be considered. To simplify the rating, let us use a point scoring system to help Mr. Y determine the best location in his office. Diagram 9.8 shows the calculations.

You will find the rating criteria of the simplified point system in the appendix of this book. The system is logically structured to help laymen calculate the most auspicious space for themselves or another person.

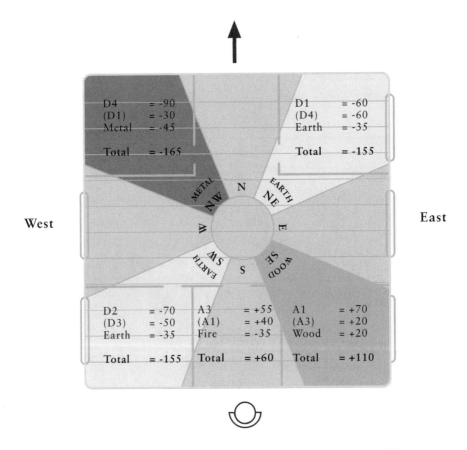

Diagram 9.8: The LI Building Trigram and the Personal Life Trigram of Mr. Y have different scores (see appendix). The elements of the directions interacting with Mr. Y's SUN Trigram (Wood element) are also assessed.

This system helps avoid making unnecessary mistakes in the selection of an auspicious space. For a consultation or during a course, an advanced version of this point system with more than twenty different factors would be used.

From Diagram 9.8, you can work out that the highest score is the south-east room with +110 points. Mr. Y will surely choose to work in this most auspicious room.

Next Mr. Y has to decide which area, within the microspace of his office, is the most auspicious place for him to sit and work. For this purpose we subdivide the office room once again according to the compass directions.

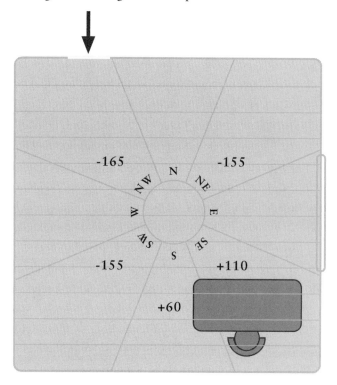

Diagram 9.9: Microspace of the south-east room with scoring points for the compass directions. The scoring is the same as for the building plan (macrospace). In the south-east room the most auspicious location for Mr. Y to sit is also the south-east sector of the room with +110 points.

CHAPTER 10
Feng Shui Golden Measurements

The so-called *Lu-Ban* ruler was the official Chinese unit of measurement for construction and was invented by the Imperial Carpenter named Gong Shu Ban who lived in the Lu State during the Warring States Period (475–221 BC).

The use of the standardized Feng Shui Golden Ruler was first mentioned during the Sung Dynasty (AD 960–1128), when it was used by the Imperial Carpenter for building official furniture, doors and windows. This Golden Ruler was created according to complicated mathematical calculations based on nature's harmonic matrix that has soothing musical tones. The measurements of the Golden Ruler, which has a length of 16¹⁵⁄₁₆ inches or 42.96 centimetres, is actually connected with the numerical factor of the earth's circumference.

The Feng Shui Golden Ruler has eight main sections and each section is further divided into four smaller subsections with a width of 0.525 of an inch or 1.34 cm. There are four auspicious sections and four inauspicious sections. A summary of the key meanings is given in Table 9.

After the eighth section, the whole length of the eight sections repeats again in the same order. If an object is longer than the Feng Shui Ruler, the ruler is repeatedly placed along the length and then the remaining section is taken where the measurement ends. Five-metre-length Golden Feng Shui measuring tapes in English are also available to measure more easily and precisely, and can be obtained from Feng Shui shops. Wrong measurements from using the short ruler can thus be avoided.

Table 9: The Sections on the Feng Shui Ruler

Section 1	Section 2
0 – 2 $\frac{1}{8}$ in (0 – 5.37 cm)	2 $\frac{1}{8}$ – 4 $\frac{1}{4}$ in (5.38 – 10.74 cm)
CHAI – Wealth	**PING – Sickness**
a) Fortune comes	a) Loss of fortune
b) Plenty of resources	b) Bad encounter with public service
c) Six harmonies and luck	c) Severe enforcement of laws and imprisonment
d) Abundant prosperity	d) Orphan, widow, widower

Section 3	Section 4
4 $\frac{1}{4}$ – 6 $\frac{3}{8}$ in (10.75 – 16.11 cm)	6 $\frac{3}{8}$ – 8 $\frac{1}{2}$ in (16.12 – 21.48 cm)
LI – Separation	**YI – Nobility and integrity**
a) Denial of wealth	a) Gain descendants
b) Money lost	b) Profitable income
c) Cheated of wealth	c) Talented offspring
d) Loss of everything	d) Very lucky and prosperous

Section 5	Section 6
8 $\frac{1}{2}$ – 10 $\frac{5}{8}$ in (21.49 – 26.85 cm)	10 $\frac{5}{8}$ – 12 $\frac{11}{16}$ in (26.86 – 32.22 cm)
KUAN – Official power	**CHIEH – Catastrophe**
a) Plenty of food	a) Death and departure
b) Side income and lottery	b) Loss of descendants
c) Improved income	c) Forced to leave ancestral home or loss of job
d) Rich and noble	d) Loss of money

Section 7	Section 8
12 $\frac{11}{16}$ – 14 $\frac{13}{16}$ in (32.23 – 37.59 cm)	14 $\frac{13}{16}$ – 16 $\frac{15}{16}$ in (37.60 – 42.96 cm)
HAI – Harm and injury	**PEN – Source or capital**
a) Disasters and calamities	a) Wealth comes
b) Possible death	b) Plenty of promotions in job
c) Attracts sickness	c) Arrival of plenty of wealth
d) Litigation and quarrels	d) Everything turns into plenty

Here is a range of auspicious measurements that can be used for the widths and heights of doors, windows, tables, furniture, etc. The measurements below are rounded to the nearest positive sections so that you will always end up in an auspicious section.

Table 10: Examples for Auspicious Measurements

Section 1 – CHAI – Wealth
0 – 2 ⅛ in (0 – 5.34 cm)
14 ⅞ – 19 in (43 cm – 48 cm)
33 ⅞ – 35 ¾ in (86 cm – 91 cm)
50 ¾ – 52 ¾ in (129 cm – 134 cm)
67 ¾ – 69 ¾ in (172 cm – 177 cm)
84 ⅝ – 86 ⅝ in (215 cm – 220 cm)
101 ½ – 103 ½ in (258 cm – 263 cm)
118 ½ – 120 ½ in (301 cm – 306 cm)
135 ⅜ – 137 ⅜ in (344 cm – 349 cm)
152 ¼ – 154 ¼ in (387 cm – 392 cm)
169 ¼ – 171 ⅛ in (430 cm – 434.5 cm)
186 ⅛ – 188 ⅛ in (473 cm – 477.5 cm)

Section 4 – YI – Nobility and integrity
6 ⅜ – 8 ⅜ in (16.5 cm – 21.5 cm)
23 ⅜ – 25 ¼ in (59.5 cm – 64 cm)
40 1/4 – 42 ¼ in (102.5 cm – 107 cm)
57 ¼ – 59 ⅛ in (145 cm – 150 cm)
74 ⅛ – 76 in (188 cm – 193 cm)
91 – 93 in (231 cm – 236 cm)
108 – 109 ¼ in (274 cm – 279 cm)
124 ⅞ – 126 ¾ in (317 cm – 322 cm)
141 ¼ – 143 ⅝ in (360 cm – 365 cm)
158 ⅝ – 160 ½ in (403 cm – 408 cm)
175 ⅝ – 177 ½ in (446 cm – 451 cm)
192 ½ – 194 ⅜ in (489 cm – 494 cm)

Section 5 – KUAN – Official power
8 ½ – 10 ⅜ in (22 cm – 26.5 cm)
25 ⅜ – 27 ⅜ in (64.5 cm – 69.5 cm)
42 ⅜ – 44 ¼ in (108 cm – 112.5 cm)
59 ¼ – 61 ¼ in (151 cm – 155.5 cm)
76 ¼ – 78 ⅛ in (194 cm – 198 cm)
93 ⅛ – 95 in (236.5 cm – 241.5 cm)
110 – 112 in (279.5 cm – 284.5 cm)
127 – 128 ⅞ in (322.5 cm – 327 cm)
143 ⅞ – 145 ¾ in (365.5 cm – 370 cm)
160 ¾ – 162 ⅝ in (408.5 cm – 413 cm)
177 ¾ – 179 ½ in (451.5 cm – 456 cm)
194 ⅝ – 196 ½ in (494.5 cm – 499 cm)

Section 8 – PEN – Source or capital
14 ⅞ – 16 ¾ in (38 cm – 42.5 cm)
31 ⅞ – 33 ¾ in (81 cm – 85.5 cm)
48 ¾ – 50 ⅝ in (124 cm – 128.5 cm)
65 ⅝ – 67 ½ in (167 cm – 171.5 cm)
82 ½ – 84 ⅜ in (209.5 cm – 214.5 cm)
99 ½ – 101 ⅜ in (252.5 cm – 257.5 cm)
116 ⅜ – 118 ¼ in (295.5 cm – 300.5 cm)
133 ¼ – 135 ⅛ in (338.5 – 343.5 cm)
150 ¼ – 152 ⅛ in (381.5 cm – 386.5 cm)
167 ⅛ – 169 in (424.5 cm – 429.5 cm)
184 – 186 in (467.5 cm – 472 cm)

Inauspicious dimensions cause disharmony

Doors and windows are symbols radiating unique frequencies according to their shape and size. When the dimensions of a door or window are auspicious, the door or window vibrates harmonic frequencies and sounds. These harmonic frequencies positively affect the people going through the door or facing the window.

Research carried out in Europe, North America, Asia and Australia confirmed that the doors of businesses with inauspicious dimensions according to the Feng Shui Ruler had adverse effects on the emotions and feelings of staff and customers.

Dimensions of windows

Windows that have negative Feng Shui dimensions cause concentration problems, especially for people who sit in front of windows.

An accounting firm in Sydney, Australia, renovated all their offices. The staff's seating arrangements were changed. In the new arrangement, six of the accounting staff had to sit facing the windows. Management found that the accounting personnel who sat facing the windows were making many accounting errors and some complained of having problems with concentration. It was discovered that the windows in front of the accounting staff had inauspicious dimensions. Remedy — the negative measurements of the windows were reduced to the next auspicious measurement by putting strips of colored tape onto the glass panels. After the remedy, the performance of the staff returned to normal.

Dimensions of doors

A medium-sized company had a history of conflicts among the staff and poor financial returns. Feng Shui remedies were carried out and profit results improved by twenty to twenty-five per cent annually over three years. But the disharmony among the staff remained. Staff relations only improved after the height of the doors was changed to auspicious measurements. At first the company had neglected to change the inauspicious dimensions of the doors, as the management considered this unimportant. The office had six doors, which all the staff used throughout the day. The size of the doors was 78¾ inches (200 centimetres), which comes under the main section *Catastrophe* (subsection *Departure* and *Death*), and the width 39⅜ inches (100 centimetres), which comes under the main section *Separation* (subsection *Cheated of Wealth*).

By using strips of wood on the door frames, reducing the size to the next auspicious dimensions, the new height for all doors was 77⅝ inches (198 centimetres) —

under the main section *Official Power* (subsection *Rich and Noble*). The width was changed to 35¼ inches (89.5 centimetres) — under the main section *Wealth* (subsection *Six Harmonies*).

Six weeks later I received a letter from the chief executive stating that staff relationships had improved and that he was surprised the dimensions of doors were so important for business premises.

How to measure doors

When measuring doors, you measure the length and width of the actual opening (see Diagrams 10.1–4).

Table 11: Examples of Auspicious Door Measurements (Height and width can be combined in any way.)	
Auspicious door dimensions are:	
Height	**Width**
76 in (193 cm)	24 ¹³/₁₆ in (63 cm)
78 in (198 cm)	27 ³/₁₆ in (69 cm)
82 ¹¹/₁₆ in (210 cm)	32 ¹/₄ in (82 cm)
85 ¹³/₁₆ in (218 cm)	35 ¹/₁₆ in (89 cm)
92 ¹⁵/₁₆ in (236 cm)	42 ¹/₈ in (107 cm)
	44 ¹/₁₆ in (112 cm)
	52 in (132 cm)
	59 ¹/₁₆ in (150 cm)
	67 ³/₄ in (172 cm)
	68 ⁷/₈ in (175 cm)

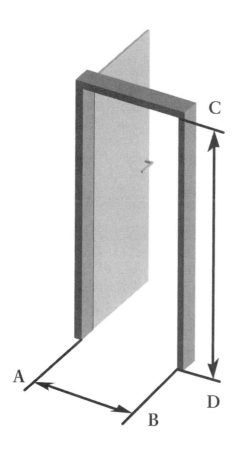

Diagram 10.1: Measuring a rectangular door. Measure A-B and C-D.

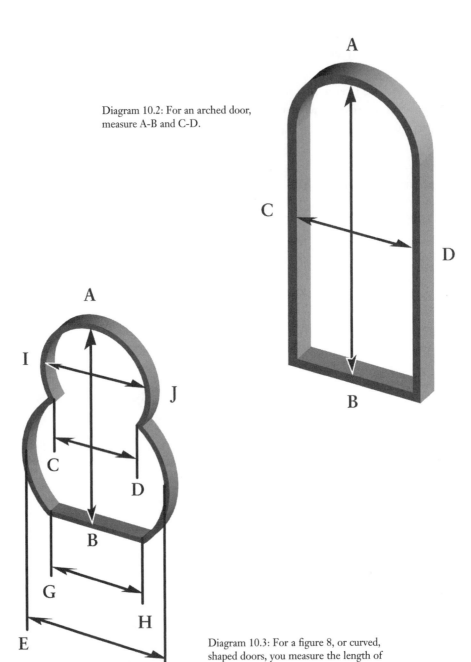

Diagram 10.2: For an arched door, measure A-B and C-D.

Diagram 10.3: For a figure 8, or curved, shaped doors, you measure the length of the longest curved area. Measure A–B, C–D, E–F, G–H and I–J.

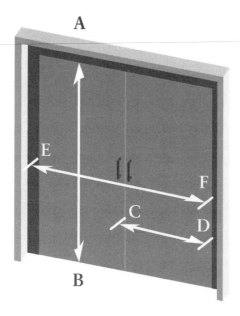

Diagram 10.4: For a double opening door, if both sides of the door open then you measure the opening spaces A–B and E–F. If only one side of the door is open regularly, and the other section only used for special occasions, you measure only the side that is open regularly. For example, you measure the height A–B and width C–D.

How to measure windows

When measuring windows, the opening of the window has to be measured first, together with the length and width of the window panels. If a window has several panels, each glass panel is measured separately (see Diagrams 10.5–9).

Auspicious dimensions for work tables and desks

Allocating auspicious dimensions for a work table is very important. When a person is working at a table for many hours each day, the dimensions of the table will affect a person's mental and emotional well-being. An inauspicious table dimension tends to cause difficulties in focusing on the work, and in these conditions a person would generally make more mistakes.

For a senior executive, the table represents his/her department or the whole company. How a company is managed can be seen by where the chief executive's table is placed, the shape of the table, its size and dimensions.

The best work table is one in the regular shape of a kidney. When you sit in front of a kidney-shaped table, you can touch the edges when you open your arms. This

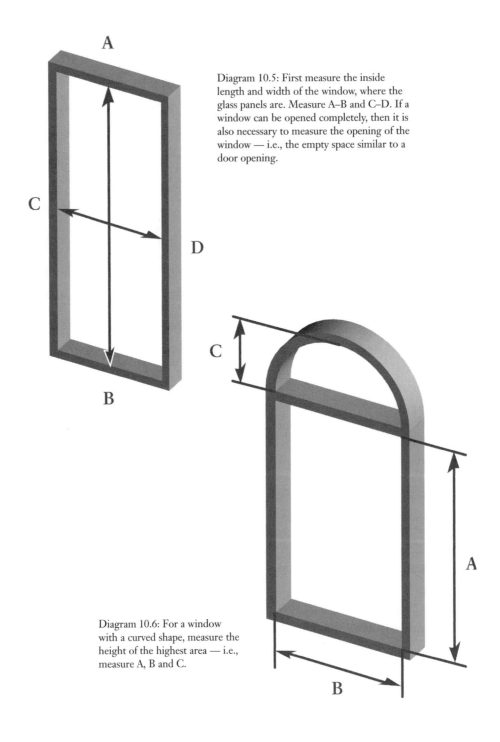

Diagram 10.5: First measure the inside length and width of the window, where the glass panels are. Measure A–B and C–D. If a window can be opened completely, then it is also necessary to measure the opening of the window — i.e., the empty space similar to a door opening.

Diagram 10.6: For a window with a curved shape, measure the height of the highest area — i.e., measure A, B and C.

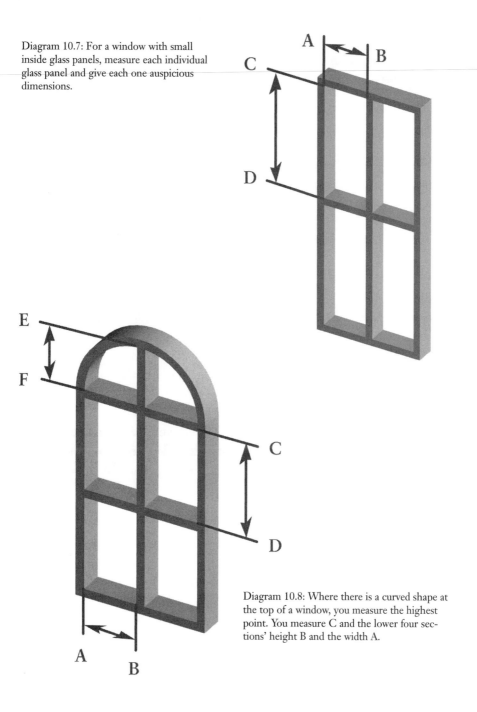

Diagram 10.7: For a window with small inside glass panels, measure each individual glass panel and give each one auspicious dimensions.

Diagram 10.8: Where there is a curved shape at the top of a window, you measure the highest point. You measure C and the lower four sections' height B and the width A.

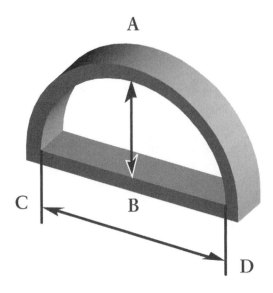

Diagram 10.9: You measure the highest point at A–B and the width C–D.

is a symbolic indication that you are in full control of the business at all times. People working at such kidney-shaped tables tend to be more humane and considerate as employers.

It is preferable for all corners of a square or rectangular table to be rounded off to avoid negative ley rays being directed aggressively from the corners that would create aggressive energy in a room.

It is most important that a work table be solid and firm to reflect business and work stability. The front and sides of a good work table should be covered to maintain the discretion of the business. Working on a fragile, wobbly table may cause the loss of the job.

How to measure a desk

The auspicious measurements of a table top are important, but the height of a work table or tables should be adjusted to individual requirements. More important than an auspicious Feng Shui measurement is a measurement for comfort so that the person sitting at the table has a straight back and relaxed breathing.

For most desk and tabletop shapes, measurements of the length and width should be taken at their widest points. Circular tops, of course, need only be measured by their radius.

An L-shape is the least-preferred shape for a work table because of its unevenness. This shape makes it more difficult for users to have control of their work or the whole business. If more desk space is required, to accommodate a telephone and a computer for example, then a separate table with its own four legs placed alongside would be preferrable to an L-shaped desk. If an L-shaped desk is unavoidable, all sides of the desk (usually five) need to be measured.

Any of the measurements shown in these tables and diagrams can be combined. You may find that some of these suggested auspicious dimensions differ from the standard measurements of door, table or window dimensions. According to my research, more than 80 per cent of office furniture in Western countries does not have auspicious dimensions. It may appear to be cheaper to use standardized furniture, but the consequences of the negative effects far outweigh any cost savings.

This is a market opportunity for a whole new industry — the manufacturing of windows, doors and office furniture according to the Feng Shui Golden measurements.

Table 12: Suggested Auspicious Dimensions for Work Tables and Desks *(length and width can be combined in any way)*	
Length	**Width**
34 ⁵⁄₈ in (88 cm)	25 ⁹⁄₁₆ in (65 cm)
44 ¹⁄₁₆ in (112 cm)	27 ³⁄₁₆ in (69 cm)
52 in (132 cm)	32 ¹⁄₄ in (82 cm)
61 ¹⁄₄ in (155 cm)	35 ¹⁄₁₆ in (89 cm)
76 in (193 cm)	42 ¹⁄₈ in (107 cm)
78 in (198 cm)	
84 ⁵⁄₈ in (215 cm)	

CHAPTER 11
Buildings and Locations to Avoid

A building for human occupation should be constructed with a solid, balanced foundation. The shape and structure of a building has to be pleasant to look at, like an attractive person's face and body.

Let your intuitive feeling guide you when selecting a building as an office or business headquarters. Choose one that you like, and one that generally gives you a good feeling. Normally, your intuitive decision will be correct. However, it is good to know about certain "building defects" that would affect your health and well-being, and that of your staff.

You can feel a building's defects in your body
In Malaysia, a five-story building was built with its left side heavy and lopsided. I noticed many office workers leaning more to the left side as I watched them walking out of the building during their lunch break. Their bodies were simulating the building's defects.

In Frankfurt, Germany, I interviewed several staff who occupied a building that had a major part of its structure missing. Eight of the ten staff I spoke to told me that they suffered from hip and back problems while working in their offices. These body parts related exactly to the missing areas of the building.

It is vitally important to select a suitable building for business premises to ensure that the staff working there experience the harmony and balance that builds a strong successful business. A Feng Shui–designed building normally has higher vitalized

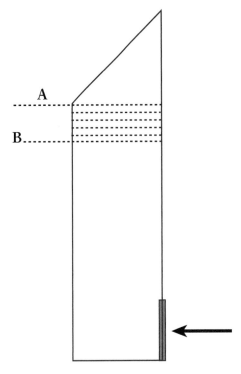

Diagram 11.1: A scalpel-shaped building. Normally the slanted roof surface should amount to less than 5 per cent of the total height of the building.

energy and is far more dynamic than other buildings. While office workers are energized during the day they perform at their best. They can work for long hours without having to drink copious cups of coffee to keep them fully awake.

A scalpel-shaped building

A scalpel-shaped building is exceptionally aggressive and threatening to neighboring buildings. The sharp apex quickly directs energy up to the top with a suction effect. Generally, people working above level A where the slant begins (see Diagram 11.1) would lose their balance and lack intuition in decision making. People who occupy spaces between level A and B would experience similar difficulties, but to a lesser degree.

There is a very high incidence of business failures worldwide in this type of scalpel-shaped building. Feng Shui remedies are imperative for such existing buildings.

Architects often complain that Feng Shui blocks their creativity in designing innovative buildings, but this is not true. This complaint comes from a general lack of knowledge of Feng Shui principles. As Feng Shui practitioners, we do not necessarily stop an aggressive architect expressing his/her inner feeling by designing a scalpel-shaped building. Businesses

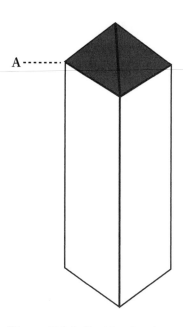

A

Diagram 11.2: In Frankfurt there is a well-known building that has a pyramid-shaped roof. Many Feng Shui experts claim that the presence of this building weakens Frankfurt as a financial center for Germany and the European Union.

that occupy the spaces in this type of building, along with the occupants, need to be protected by balancing remedies. If a scalpel-shaped building is threatening its neighbors, the necessary Feng Shui remedies should be implemented.

The knife-shaped Bank of China building in Hong Kong has a similar effect, and is supposedly showing a political point of view. It symbolized China's displeasure towards the British colonial power. The health of three British governors was severely affected after its completion. Now colonial rule is over, this building should be redesigned, as it is a threat to the city of Hong Kong.

Buildings with a pyramid roof

Many modern buildings have a pyramid-shaped roof. A pyramid-shaped roof is a very negative symbol for a commercial building. Pyramids were used in South America and China in ancient times to preserve food, and were used for medical treatments and rituals. In ancient Egypt and in China special chambers in pyramids were used to preserve the mummies of the royal family before burial. Therefore a pyramid also represents aspects of a mortuary.

A pyramid is one of the symbols that create "attacks" on people and animals. A person's immune system becomes weak just by looking at a pyramid. Many scientific experiments verify this negative effect.

A pyramid roof tends to suck up more energy to its apex. People working in such a building, especially those occupying the

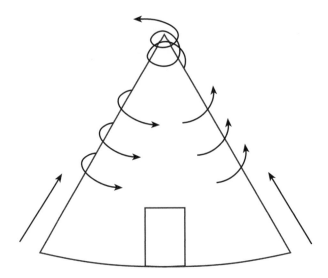

Diagram 11.3: A cone- or snail-shaped building generates a special swing of energy that is moving upwards to its peak.

pyramid area and the five floors closest to level A (see Diagram 11.2) of the pyramid roof, would have a feeling that they are being lifted upwards and tend to lose their grounding and balance. Business failures are exceptionally high in such buildings. Suitable remedies would need to be carried out by a very skilled Feng Shui consultant.

Cone-shaped buildings

A cone- or snail-shaped building generates a special swing of energy that is moving upwards to its peak. People occupying such a building tend to feel its spinning effect. While this type of building can be acceptable for fantasy and fun, it is exceptionally unsuitable for business premises or for government departments. There is a high incidence of business failures in these buildings, mainly due to a lack of balance and general disorientation. Feng Shui remedies must be carried out otherwise the cost to the business is exceptionally high. Without remedies, this type of building could eventually end up as a relic — empty, as everything is moving up. (An American Indian tipi has only a partial cone shape. Due to the opening on top the energy flow is more positive.)

The new German Parliament House in Berlin also has a cone-shaped interior design element pointing downwards. Unfortunately, this is very inauspicious for a building where laws are constituted.

Glass-walled buildings

To create better lighting, many modern buildings are designed with more than 70 per cent of the outer walls made of glass. Glass-walled buildings, however, promote a feeling of fear and insecurity and of being exposed without protection. Glass-walled buildings leak a lot of energy; the Qi and oxygen in a glass building generally tend to be very low. Glass-walled buildings are also expensive to build and clean. Despite more incoming light, the vital energy in a glass building is very low. There is a higher incidence of bankruptcies and reduced profits for businesses that occupy glass-walled buildings. It is exceptionally costly to carry out Feng Shui remedies.

There is another negative aspect: commercial buildings need stability and an element of secrecy that a glass building cannot offer. That is why all major bank buildings are solidly built to instill stability and strength — compared to a building made from glass.

Some commercial buildings may be designed with glass walls but special design skills based on Feng Shui are necessary to ensure that a building is stable and also able to avoid any possible leakage of cosmic Qi and oxygen.

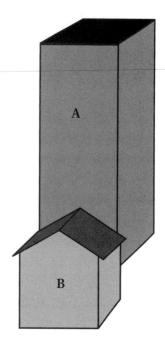

Diagram 11.4: This type of situation occurs quite often in towns and cities. The high building A "suppresses" and "attacks" building B, especially if the shadow of building A is cast over building B for more than a few hours a day. The occupants of building B would tend to be more depressed and pessimistic in their outlook. On the other hand, A gives building B a very solid backing and support to enhance success.

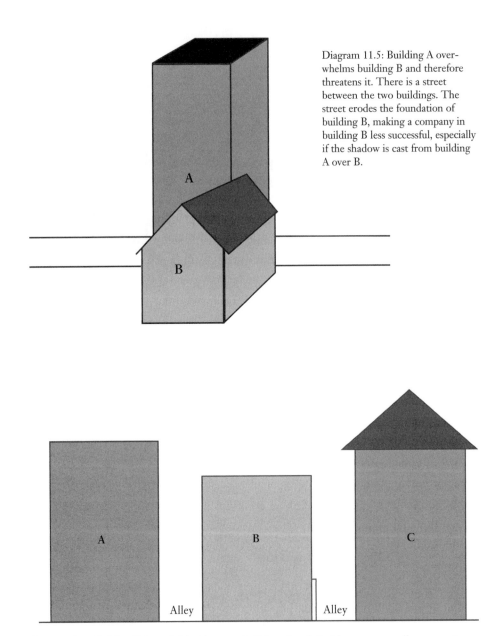

Diagram 11.5: Building A over-whelms building B and therefore threatens it. There is a street between the two buildings. The street erodes the foundation of building B, making a company in building B less successful, especially if the shadow is cast from building A over B.

Diagram 11.6: Building B is sandwiched between buildings A and C with two narrow alleys separating them. The front entrance to building B is overpowered and blocked by building C. The wall of building C symbolizes an obstacle for the occupants of building B. The companies in building B would tend to face many obstacles in their daily work even though building A provides a backing.

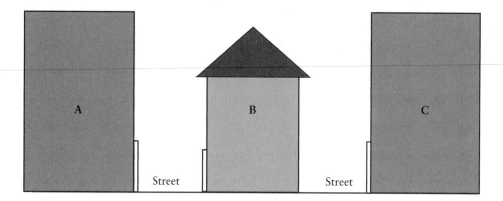

Diagram 11.7: Building B is between buildings A and C which are separated by two streets. Therefore building B is not blocked by building A or C. However, building B has a street immediately behind it and therefore lacks a good backing necessary for sustaining consistent long-term success, especially during difficult economic times. The situation for building B would improve if the street behind it had infrequent traffic. Ideally, no road, street or water should be immediately behind a building, as they severely weaken the backing.

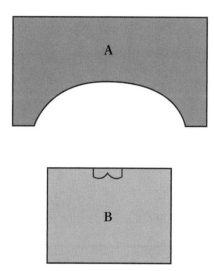

Diagram 11.8: Building A is embracing and drawing the energy from building B across the square. If both buildings are used as retail shops, then building B would lose many customers to building A. However, if there is a street between them, then the negative effects are lessened.

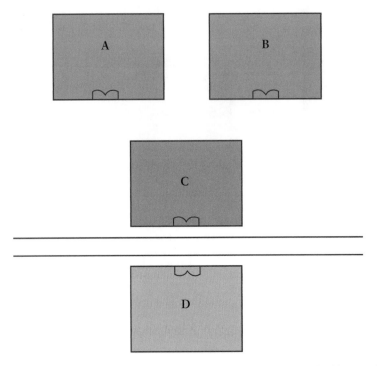

Diagram 11.9: Buildings A, B and C together form a triangular shape, threatening building D. If building D is a retail shop, it may lose many customers. Building C is the best choice of all four buildings, as it receives support from buildings A and B.

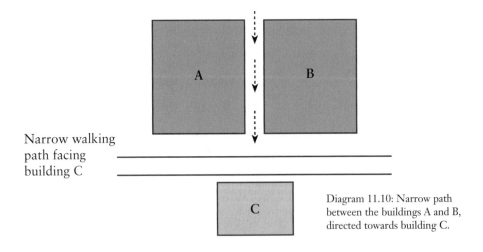

Narrow walking path facing building C

Diagram 11.10: Narrow path between the buildings A and B, directed towards building C.

Tunnel and suction effects

The type of condition shown in Diagram 11.10 can often be seen in big cities and other congested areas. There is a narrow walking path between buildings A and B, creating a tunnel effect that directs an attacking wind to the front of building C. The strong wind "splits" building C in the middle. The wind becomes more aggressive if building C is facing the sea, a lake or a mountain range. Normally businesses in building C would not do well. Unfortunately there are no effective remedies to neutralize this type of aggressive wind condition for the ground floor. Windshields can be installed in front of windows on higher floors to divert the strong wind.

T-junction and cul-de-sac

If a business building faces a T-junction or cul-de-sac that is within 165 to 230 feet (50 to 70 metres), this is very inauspicious.

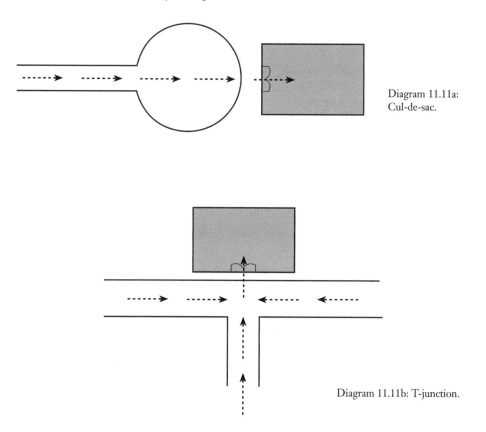

Diagram 11.11a:
Cul-de-sac.

Diagram 11.11b: T-junction.

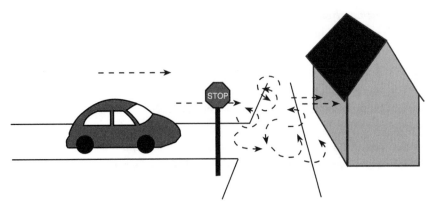

Diagram 11.11c: Energy movements at a T-junction.

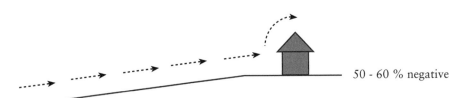

50 - 60 % negative

Diagram 11.12a: Uphill cul-de-sac and T-junction.

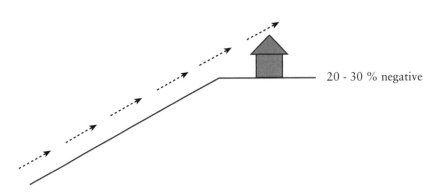

20 - 30 % negative

Diagram 11.12b: It is less negative when a cul-de-sac or a T-junction is moving uphill.

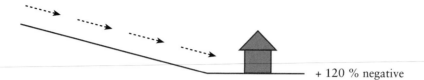

Diagram 11.12c: A downhill cul-de-sac and T-junction has a far more negative effect.

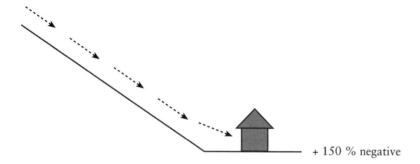

Diagram 11.12d: The safe distance for a building is between 300 and 450 feet (100 and 150 metres) from a downhill cul-de-sac. This location is dangerous; most businesses fail within three years.

In Feng Shui a cul-de-sac means *end of the path* for prosperity and abundance. If you want to be successful, you must move out. For a business that is situated at the top of a T-junction, the head-on vehicle traffic tends to be very busy. Depending on the traffic, the building is exposed to dust and fumes from the approaching cars. This causes severe health problems among employees, who cannot relax and be friendly, resulting in bad customer relations. Customers tend to get more nervous and are in a hurry. It is not very likely that they will be in the mood to, as the saying goes, "shop 'til they drop."

From my personal experience I have never seen a successful business or shopping mall that is directly facing a busy cul-de-sac or T-junction. Shops and business premises in these situations tend to be run-down, and shopkeepers also tend to be more depressed or sick if they work there for more than six months.

Always remember: in business you have a choice and the opportunity of having good business premises, if you set your mind and heart to find them. Even if you have to incur higher costs, avoid situating your business at the end of a cul-de-sac or a T-junction.

A building "falling into the sea"

Another type of building you should avoid is a building that has the sea, a lake, a river, a cliff, or a busy road to the rear. Think of a building as if you are sitting on a chair with a strong backrest to support you. Without it, you would fall when you lean backwards.

Water or heavy traffic to the rear, within one width of a building, slowly erodes the foundation and stability of the building and the business inside. In Feng Shui we call this *mountain falling into the sea*, which is very inauspicious for business premises. The water energy at the back also attracts cosmic Qi and oxygen, thereby depriving the business premises of the Qi energy.

A cliff more than sixteen feet (five metres) high should be at least three hundred feet (one hundred metres) from any building.

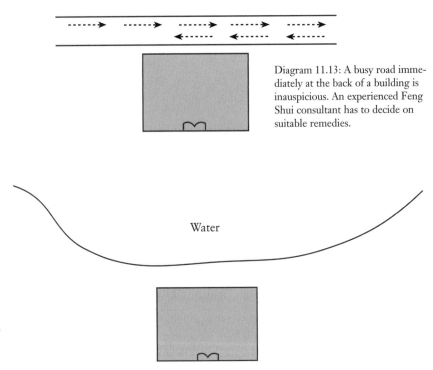

Diagram 11.13: A busy road immediately at the back of a building is inauspicious. An experienced Feng Shui consultant has to decide on suitable remedies.

Water

Diagram 11.14: Plenty of water within 165 feet (50 metres) of the back of a building is most inauspicious.

CHAPTER 12
"Attacking" and Inauspicious Structures

A building represents all people who occupy its spaces. It gives protection and safety to its occupants. In Feng Shui practice, it is very important to observe and study the features and structures of buildings within 330 feet (100 metres) of your building's immediate external environment. Any objects, structures or other buildings nearby that are aggressive in design or features will affect all occupants in the building.

To prove these effects, tests were carried out in twenty countries, both in the West and the East, on people who had no idea what Feng Shui is. So there was no question of bias or of anyone being unduly influenced by their belief systems.

The tests were carried out using electrograph, cardiograph, and other biofeedback devices to check the muscle response and immune sensitivity of people occupying buildings that are the object of an "attack" by an adjacent building. There was one consistent result: All occupants were under tremendous stress and, when tested, their muscular systems and limbs were weak.

The illustrations given in this chapter show inauspicious structures and buildings outside business premises that have negative effects on a building's occupants. These examples describe the physical, mental and emotional health problems of the affected occupants. No remedies are suggested here, for these problems are major ones that require the skill of experienced Feng Shui consultants who can offer solutions.

A substantial number of these businesses would become bankrupt within five years unless Feng Shui remedies were carried out. These are the types of buildings you should avoid renting or buying, to avoid unnecessary stress, health problems and financial loss for you and your staff.

Harmful energies from the corner of a building

Attacks from neighboring buildings can severely affect the business, as can be seen in the diagrams below.

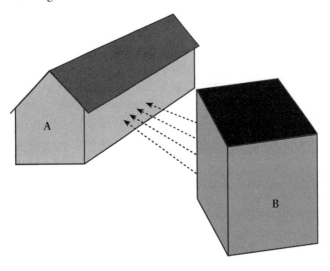

Diagram 12.1: Building B is a high-rise building with a sharp corner that directs overwhelming and harmful energies to the center area of building A, as if to cut building A in half. As a result of this harmful energy, the occupants of building A would tend to have back pains and feel extremely fearful.

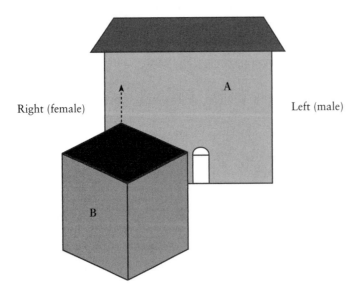

Right (female)

Left (male)

Diagram 12.2: Building A is threatened by the harmful energies of the sharp corner of building B. These harmful energies are directed to the female side, and are on the front representing the right side of the face (to determine the female side, imagine you are standing at the front door looking out). In these conditions, office workers, especially the female workers in building A, would tend to suffer from facial problems on their right side. Office workers in building A would also tend to be more nervous.

Diagram 12.3: An "attack" by two buildings. An overwhelming force of harmful energies from the corners of buildings B and C is directed at building A. Most companies would become unprofitable and fail within three years of moving into building A.

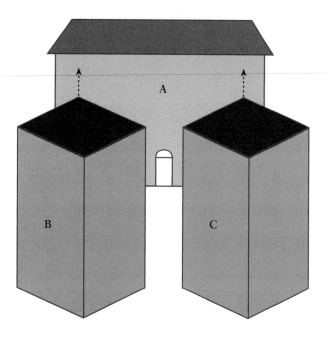

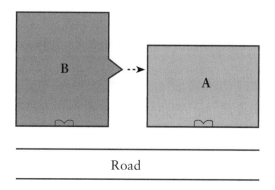

Road

Diagram 12.4: Building B is directing harmful energies to the right side of building A, and is thereby creating health problems for people working there.

Diagram 12.5: Building B symbolically attacks the right shoulder of building A. People working in this building may suffer from shoulder problems. The effect is less aggressive if the road has heavy traffic.

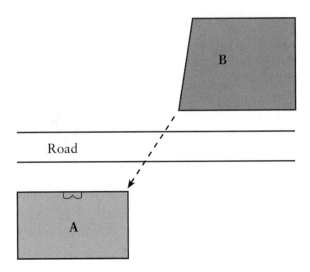

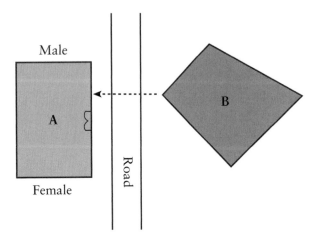

Diagram 12.6: Building B is directing harmful energies towards the left front of building A. The left side of a building (imagine yourself standing in the entrance door facing outside) represents the male. Therefore the front and the faces of all the occupants in building A, especially any males, are symbolically attacked and weakened. The attack would cause irritation and concentration problems.

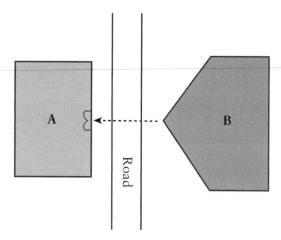

Diagram 12.7: In this case building A receives a frontal attack from B.

In Diagram 12.7, building B looks like an arrowhead. All the energy of building B, together with its occupants, constitutes a symbolic attack on the entrance (the mouth) of building A. As building B is a larger building than A, the attack is overwhelming.

Never move into building A, even though building B may be a smaller building. A direct attack by a building into the entrance (mouth) of another building is really lethal. It weakens the heart of all occupants, especially senior personnel. There would tend to be a higher incidence of heart attack and brain hemorrhage amongst the top management occupying building A. Many of the occupants of building A would also be extremely aggressive (because they are under attack), and unable to concentrate or make sound decisions.

From my experience and observation of situations similar to building A, businesses in this type of building would show a downturn in profit and performance, with possible failure within three years. There is also a good possibility that one of the heads of the businesses in the building could die early.

Even though you would expect many buildings to be attacked by the corners of neighboring buildings in congested cities, you have to distinguish between more or less severe and dangerous attacks.

If you are already occupying a type of building like A in Diagrams 12.4–7, then a relatively simple and cheap way to remedy the problem is to install mirrors or reflective foil shields on a section of the wall directly opposite the corner that is directing

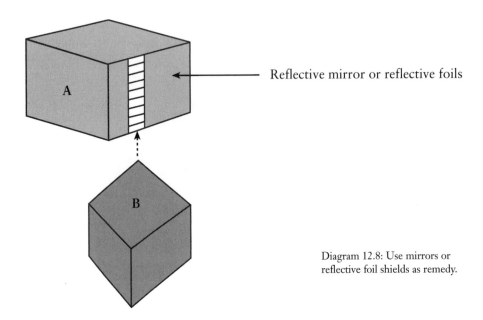

Reflective mirror or reflective foils

Diagram 12.8: Use mirrors or reflective foil shields as remedy.

the harmful energies. If windows are directly opposite this attacking line you can place mirrors in the windows or just cover the glass on the windows with reflective foil or mirrors.

Determining the exact location of obstacles

Before construction of a commercial building, architects should visit a site to familiarize themselves with the land and the shape of adjacent buildings. Special note should be taken of any harmful symbols and obstacles in the immediate vicinity. It is also suggested that they take a compass to determine the exact location of the negative symbols or obstacles. To obtain the exact location of a negative obstacle, they should stand at the geometric center of the proposed building and take the compass reading.

Once the exact direction of the harmful energy is known, an architect can provide suitable Feng Shui remedies in his or her design to counter or negate the harmful effect of the attacking corner of building B. Diagrams 12.10 and 12.11 show remedies that your architect can incorporate into the building design.

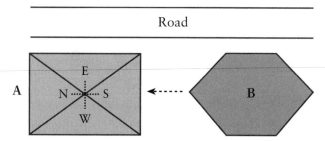

Diagram 12.9: From the central point of the proposed building, take an accurate reading of the attacking corner of building B. In this illustration, the compass reading, south 180 degrees, shows the direction from which the harmful energy of the sharp corner of building B is coming.

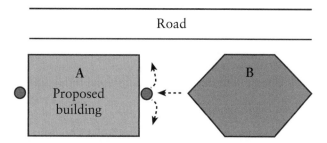

Diagram 12.10: Two large, round, shiny pillars or highly reflective steel decorations are installed immediately opposite and as high as building B's attacking corner, to deflect the negative energy.

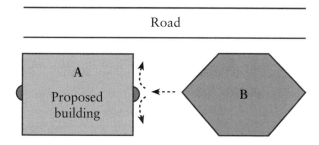

Diagram 12.11: A semi-circular shiny projection is added to both sides of building A. It could be used as a rubbish chute or a covering for drains and wastepipes.

Further examples of buildings to avoid

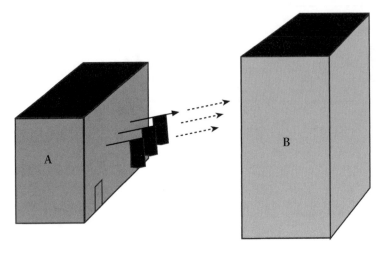

Diagram 12.12: The flagpoles on the façade of building A threaten building B. These sharp poles are like rapid arrows shot at building B. The worst hit are those who occupy the floor that directly faces the sharp poles. Occupants of building B would tend to be more nervous and often experience phantom fear.

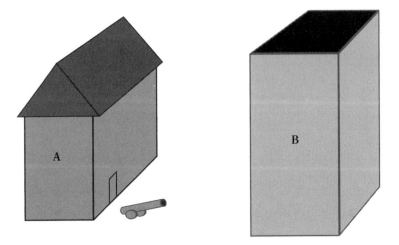

Diagram 12.13: The cannon in front of building A threatens building B. When a cannon, even if it is symbolic, is facing a building, then it directs a symbolic attack with a blast like a cannon. If the front of building B faces the cannon, then the occupants would suffer neurological and mental health problems. The business would experience a reduction in profits as very few customers would want to shop in building B. It may be difficult for some business people to believe that this constitutes a lethal weapon. However, do not underestimate the effect.

Diagram 12.14: Satellite dishes are a
common sight. The satellite dishes on
building A are pointing and beaming
harmful ley energies towards building B.
These large volumes of radiation permeate building B causing many health
problems to its occupants.

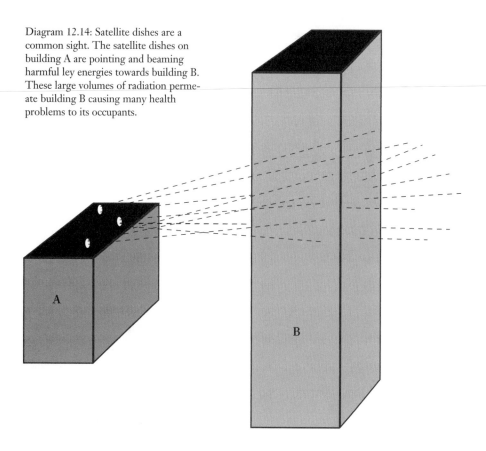

Diagram 12.15: The sharp shape of
the "Fire" window facade on this
building directs harmful energies
towards the windows of an opposite
building if they are in line. Occupants
in the opposite building, in the room
that receives the direct attack from
these A-shaped "Fire" windows,
would tend to have a higher incidence
of eye problems. Sharp A-shaped
windows are a symbol of aggression
and were used in ancient times to
block the entry of a thief or unwanted
persons. A dome or a flat window on
the façade is more welcoming and a
preferred design feature.

Attacks from posts and tree trunks

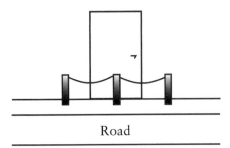

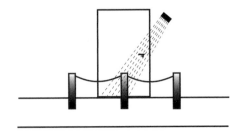

Diagram 12.16a: A seemingly harmless safety chain fence directing harmful energies towards the front door of a business entrance.

Diagram 12.16b: Remedy for Diagram 12.16a — a concave mirror.

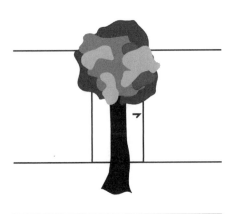

Diagram 12.17a: A robust tree blocking the front door of a restaurant.

I observed an interesting case similar to the one in Diagrams 12.16a-b. Within three years three businesses had moved out of the building, in spite of the fact that the store is situated on a busy tourist street. All the other stores on either side of this site were successful.

Diagram 12.17a shows the front door of a restaurant in the city of Lucerne, Switzerland. A robust tree with an exposed straight trunk is blocking the entrance and directing harmful energies. This restaurant, although serving very good food, had few customers. I was told that many businesses had failed in this building. However, another restaurant about 165 feet (50 metres) further along the same road had many customers and a long line waiting for seats.

I used applied kinesiology techniques to test several people who entered this

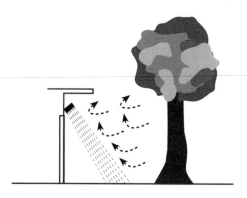

Diagram 12.17b: A 6-inch/15-cm concave mirror is installed to reflect the harmful energies radiated by the tree.

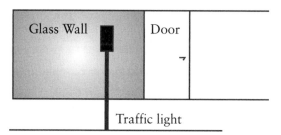

Diagram 12.18: The post of a traffic light is attacking the building.

restaurant with the tree in front. I found that the immune systems of these people became weak after they had come in. I also used a biofeedback machine and found blood pressure and heartbeat had increased — indicating that their bodies tried to protect themselves from the energy line of the tree trunk.

Normally you cannot simply remove a government-installed sign post, traffic light or trees. A common remedy is to install a six-inch (fifteen-centimetre) concave mirror above the front door towards the side facing the obstruction. Direct the mirror towards the floor in front of the obstacle to distort and reflect the harmful energy lines. If the entrance has a glass front or windows on the side, the mirror should preferably be placed in a window. An indoor mirror does not require frequent polishing to maintain its effectiveness.

A new traffic light was installed in front of a retail store regularly visited by its customers in Hamburg, Germany. However, within two years the business had lost many customers and had to close down. The harmful energy from the traffic light post is directed through the glass wall at the shop. If the wall had been made of bricks or concrete, there would have been no negative effect.

How attacking structures affect bigger buildings

Whether it is from a small retail shop or a large commercial building, from symbols or other negative environmental features, any negative energy affects the survival of the business concerned as well as the health of the occupants.

The Feng Shui problems are slightly different for a large shopping mall, or a large office building of more than three storeys where there are many different businesses under different management and ownership:

> *When a large office building or shopping mall is affected negatively by outside features, customers may not want to enter the building.*

> *In a multi-business and multi-ownership building, the negative aspects causing the health problems of the occupants are more widely spread over many people. The negative effects may take a longer time, often spreading over several years before they are fully experienced. That is the reason why, when you observe buildings that are adversely affected by outside negative features, some businesses have closed down while the majority of businesses and shops inside still appear to be successful. In these circumstances, the occupants with weaker body constitutions experienced the results of the negative effects faster.*

For offices and non-retail businesses that normally do not depend on customers coming in to their premises, it may take several years to feel any negative effects. However long it takes — there is no escape.

When an office or store within building or shopping mall is attacked by negative symbols and features within the building, the effects are much more pronounced. A square pillar in front of the entrance to a store in a mall, for example, adversely affects the health of the owner and staff. Customers intuitively sense the harmful energies directed towards them from the pillar and therefore do not enter the premises.

Attacking pillars

Five years ago, I was asked to observe for several days a very attractive shopping mall on the Gold Coast of Australia (let's call it Mall A). This shopping mall was adjacent to another shopping mall (Mall B) that did not have such a beautiful front. However, out of every ten customers walking towards the two malls, only two to three people would go into Mall A, and the other seven to eight people would go into Mall B.

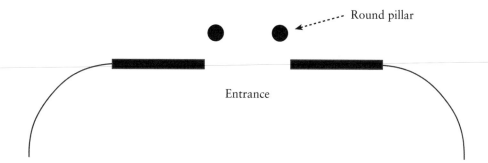

Diagram 12.19a: Entrance area of shopping center A (as seen from above).

The obstacles were two large, round, supporting pillars standing at the front entrance of Mall A. The pillars not only partially blocked the main entrance, they were also a symbolic attack that blocked the "mouth" of the building (see diagram below).

Correcting the negative effects of pillars

For a remedial Feng Shui experiment I installed two temporary concave mirrors as shown in Diagram 12.20 to distort the negative effects of the two aggressive pillars. Within an hour I noticed that the number of customers going into Mall A had increased by 30–40 per cent.

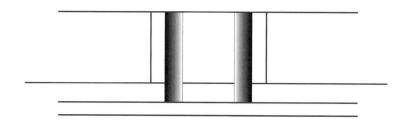

Diagram 12.19b: Front view showing two supporting pillars that are directing harmful energies that block the main entrance to Mall A.

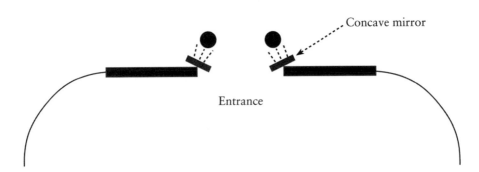

Diagram 12.20: The remedy for 12.19a — two concave mirrors with a diameter of 6 inches/15 centimetres are pointing at the feet of the pillars to neutralize their negative energy lines. I told my client to hang the mirrors inside, behind the windows. Then the mirrors do not get dirty fast and lose their effectiveness.

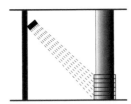

Diagram 12.21: The concave mirror causes distortion to the pillar, thereby eliminating the negative effects.

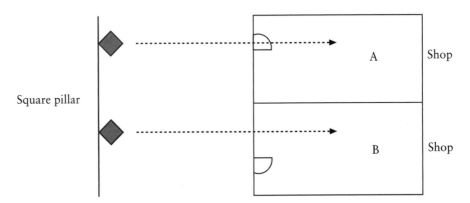

Diagram 12.22: If the wall in front of the store is made of clear glass, the harmful energy of the square pillar is directed through the glass at the store, the owner and the sales clerks.

As a general guideline, a transparent glass wall is not considered to be a solid wall. Harmful energy lines of outside attacking features can therefore penetrate from outside. If the wall in front (at least in the area of the attacking features) is made of solid materials such as brick or concrete, then the effect of any harmful energies is minimal. A round pillar is also known to direct some harmful energies but they are less negative than those from the sharp corners of a square pillar.

Several remedies can be used to block harmful ley energy within the shop as well. A piece of board can be placed in front of the attacking corner. Several natural quartz crystals, three times the size of an adult thumb, can be hung in the window at one-yard (one-metre) intervals along the whole length and immediately facing the direction of the corner attack. Alternatively, a mirror can be placed facing the pillar to deflect its harmful energy, if the pillar is not close to the entrance. Otherwise the mirror would deflect beneficial Qi energy.

I have found many similar types of obstacles and negative symbols adversely affecting businesses in many countries. Customers are intuitively very wary of these features. These types of seemingly harmless symbols and obstacles are common sights in our modern, congested business environment. They have caused many good businesses and capable, talented business people to fail — a failure no school of business or business guru can explain.

Attacking structures

The above mentioned attacks are summarized below in order of severity:

> *The entrance is attacked by another building.*

> *The front of a building is attacked by another building.*

> *The back of a building is attacked by another building causing a weakening of backing and possible business failures.*

> *The side of the building is attacked by another building. If the attack is across a busy street with heavy traffic, or the attacking building is at least 285 to 325 feet (90 to 100 metres) away, the severity is less.*

> *A second, less severe attack on a building comes from straight poles, lampposts, bus stands, road traffic lights and straight tree trunks in the door line or in front of a glass wall.*

Attacking and inauspicious structures inside office or business

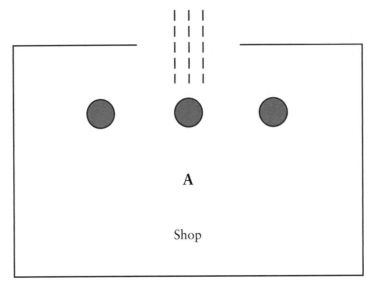

Diagram 12.23a: The harmful energy line directed from pillar A is blocking the entry of customers into the shop.

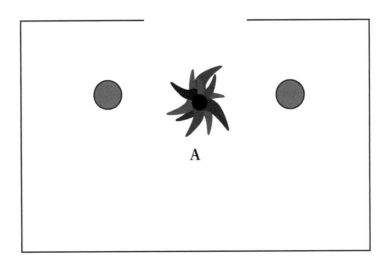

Diagram 12.23b: Remedy for Diagram 12.23a — place an attractive decoration in front of pillar A.

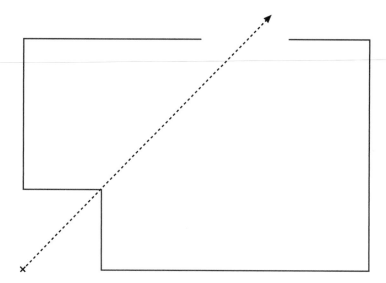

Diagram 12.24: The sharp corner marked X is directing harmful energies to customers as they enter. Furthermore, a missing corner in any business premises is basically inauspicious. The sharp corner can be remedied by placing a piece of wood, a decoration or screen in front of it. The attacking energy is strongest in the bisector area of the corner.

Diagram 12.25a: Sharp-edged corner.   Diagram 12.25b: Round-edged corner.

Everything we see in nature — like rocks, tree trunks, animals or the human body — is curved or round in shape. Humans through a long period of evolution have learned to accept anything that is curved and round as positive. Anything that is straight and sharp — like a spear, knife, or a sharp edge — is perceived to be threatening or dangerous.

Sharp corners and sharp edges are generally more threatening and create beams of negative energies. A working environment with many sharp corners on walls, cupboards, tables and shelves creates more aggressive harmful Qi and is a less favorable environment in which to work (see diagram below).

Case study

A financial consultant in New York worked in the office in Diagram 12.26a. He suffered from daily headaches and fatigue. His health was deteriorating. After the design of the office was altered by installing new, more rounded furniture, and using some specific Feng Shui remedies, his headaches and fatigue disappeared. His performance has improved substantially.

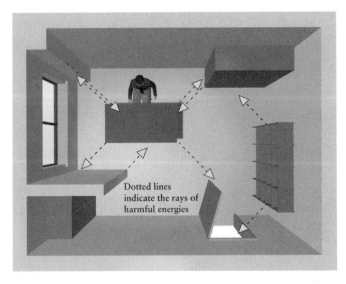

Dotted lines indicate the rays of harmful energies

Diagram 12.26a: An office with many sharp corners generating lots of aggressive and harmful beams of energy. Lots of turbulent energies usually cause so much stress that they undermine decision making.

Diagram 12.26b: All harmful ley energies are eliminated in this office with the introduction of furniture and fittings with rounded corners, creating a smooth, caressing energy flow, one that is more conducive to a harmonious and less stressful working environment.

Overhead beams

Exposed overhead beams are common in many modern offices, especially those occupying the ground floor.

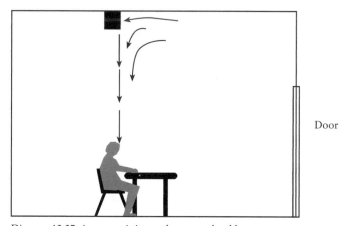

Door

Diagram 12.27: A person sitting under an overhead beam.

Its strong downward pressure affects a person sitting immediately below an overhead beam. The energy coming down from the edge of the beam also directs aggressive harmful energy downwards, causing unnecessary stress, thereby negatively affecting performance.

I was asked by the chief executive of a large German corporation to determine why he suffered severe migraines whenever he worked in his office. When he travelled and worked in other offices, he did not have any migraines. His workplace was located directly under an overhead beam. I recommended that a ceiling be placed to conceal an exposed beam in his office. This was done, and the chief executive's health problem disappeared.

Inauspicious floor plans

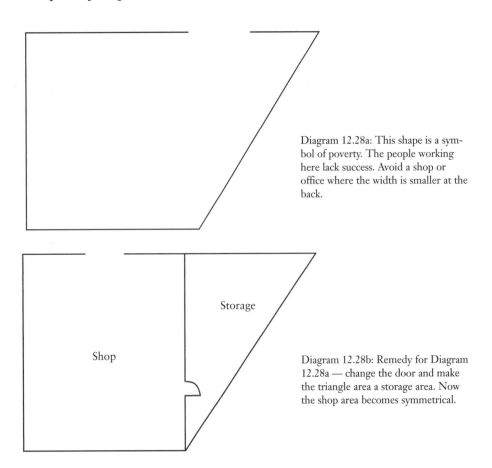

Diagram 12.28a: This shape is a symbol of poverty. The people working here lack success. Avoid a shop or office where the width is smaller at the back.

Diagram 12.28b: Remedy for Diagram 12.28a — change the door and make the triangle area a storage area. Now the shop area becomes symmetrical.

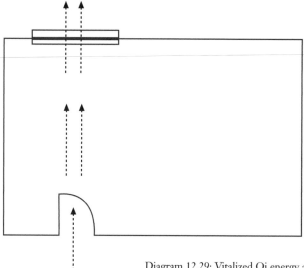

Diagram 12.29: Vitalized Qi energy and oxygen is lost when a door faces a window or a wall that is completely made of glass.

Glass at the back of the shop or office

In Business Feng Shui, a shop or an office with a glass wall at its back is considered to have a weak backing and therefore lacks support from staff and clients. It is estimated that 80 per cent of these businesses will fail within three years from the resulting lack of support from clients and bankers.

An arrangement like the one in Diagram 12.29 can often be found in modern offices. Occupants have health problems and cannot concentrate in order to make good decisions.

Other suggested Feng Shui remedies to prevent leakage of Qi energy:

› *Place a large bushy plant (at least three feet or one metre high) between the door and window.*

› *Place a divider between the door and the window.*

› *Place a set of wind chimes (the longest chime one foot/thirty centimetres long) one foot (thirty centimetres) from the door and the window.*

› *Place a natural quartz crystal (tumbler or cut crystal with smooth surface, three times the size of an adult thumb) in the middle of a large window.*

› *Replace part of the glass wall with a strong, solid wall. Place a twenty-inch/half-metre-high piece of smooth rock in front of the solid wall. Alternatively, a large picture of a mountain range can be used to give strong symbolic support and backing. Using this type of remedy, a business with a prosperity and success factor of thirty to forty per cent can be raised to eighty to ninety per cent. This normally means that a struggling business can be turned around and become profitable.*

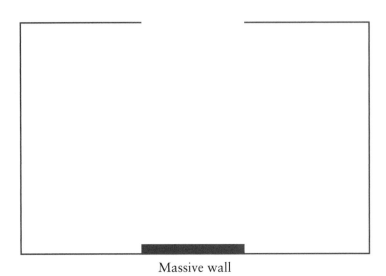

Massive wall

Diagram 12.30: Feng Shui remedies for glass walls.

Floor patterns and symbols

The symbols we see on the floor of a building, on walking areas in a shopping mall or public square, are expressions and manifestations of the designer's inner feelings or intent. Often the patterns follow a particular trend that is popular at the time or a design that personally appeals to the designer. Consequently, the energetic effect of designs is usually overlooked as the visual impression is being emphasized. Patterns and symbols used according to Feng Shui principles can otherwise enhance the energy of a space.

My investigations into the floor patterns in the Western world have shocked me. Most floor patterns and symbols are designed and placed more for a trend than for a specific purpose. Some patterns on floors actually discourage customers from going into certain shops. I am sure this was not the conscious intention.

Certain symbols can be incorporated into the floor pattern to attract and lead people into a certain area or convey symbolically that you are not welcome into an area or office for security reasons. Many shopping malls and shops are using colored footprint patterns on the floor; although this is a very practical idea, it is a rather crude one. There are many other subtle patterns that can be utilized and still give the desired effect practically and visually. This book can only show the basic principles; I provide more detailed information in my courses. Some examples of floor patterns are given below to illustrate certain effects.

Horizontal movement patterns on floors

A vertical moving pattern is good for the foyer and entrance of a shopping mall, but it is not suitable throughout the premises. This pattern moves Qi energy and oxygen very fast and can encourage people to move too quickly. In a shopping area this does not always make sense, as customers should move quickly into the retail area and, once there, move slowly as they take their time to shop, and not be taken away by irritating floor patterns. A skilful mixture of horizontal (Diagram 12.31) and vertical movement patterns (Diagram 12.37) would be ideal for this purpose.

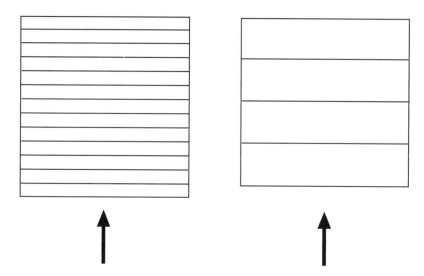

Diagram 12.31: A pattern commonly used in business premises. Horizontal stripes placed very close together indicate you cannot go forward, you are not welcome, or you can only move forward slowly and with restraint. They also slow down the inflow of beneficial Qi energy and oxygen if placed in front of a doorway or in a foyer.

Diagram 12.32: The horizontal pattern is wider than the previous one. It indicates that you are not welcome. You may move forward slowly.

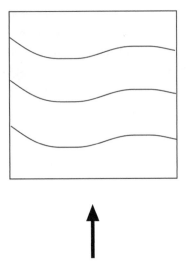

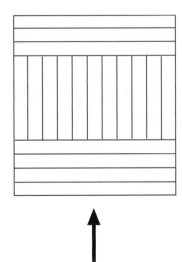

Diagram 12.33: You move along the wavy line to the edge and, if you insist, you can move forward slowly. Many people unconsciously follow the curvy line and either fall down or walk into objects placed on the side.

Diagram 12.34: Beware, your movement is closely watched! This pattern indicates that your forward movements are being controlled. If you insist, you can move to the vertical line section and be scrutinized and then move on slowly. This pattern is not suitable for a retail business. It is acceptable for financial institutions and banks. However, if this pattern is placed on stairs, it is helpful in reducing accidents.

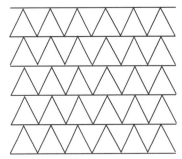

Diagram 12.35: A zigzag pattern conveys the message that you are not welcome to enter. If you insist, you can come through the area marked by the inverted pointed arrows.

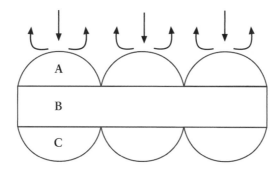

Diagram 12.36: This arched pattern suggests that you "Hold back!" You can take your time to go through, but watch your step. Once you have entered area A, you can go to area B and then to area C, where you will be embraced and welcomed wholeheartedly.

Diagram 12.37: This is a vertical moving pattern. This floor symbol indicates to you to go right in as fast as you can.

Readers can adopt the principles illustrated in this chapter to locate good offices or shops. It is disturbing to see enterprising businesses fail because of Feng Shui problems that are beyond the control of business operators. It is hoped that as more business people become familiar with Feng Shui principles, they will in turn have more harmonious, user-friendly commercial premises designed.

CHAPTER 13
Harmful Earth and Room Energies

An empty room is like an open field. However, once you place furniture, carpets, technical equipment and other fixtures, you create obstacles and introduce many types of energy. Special types of energy are also produced by the interaction of materials used in the construction of the room. Furthermore, various types of earth energy from below the ground also radiate up into the room.

If the room is enclosed with little ventilation, it tends to affect adversely the health and performance of the people working there. In this chapter, I will highlight some of the health-damaging energies and their effects. I will also explain about structures in the immediate environment and how they can affect your performance.

Geopathic stress rays

These types of aggressive stress rays are generally created by underground running water. Depending on the building structure and building materials, these rays can gather and multiply more energies as they move upwards into the upper floors. These geopathic stress rays are even found in high-rise buildings on the fiftieth floor!

Over the last few years, the managers of fifteen large corporations, including several multinational corporations, have asked me to investigate and explain why they had problems maintaining their company's profitability. In sixty per cent of these investigations, their top executives were sitting over geopathic stress rays caused by underground water (see Diagrams 13.1–3). Twenty per cent of the top executives sat over stress areas caused by so-called "black streams," which will be explained later in this chapter. In another ten per cent of cases, the offices had very bad Feng Shui. Only in the remaining ten per cent were the problems attributed to management and outdated products.

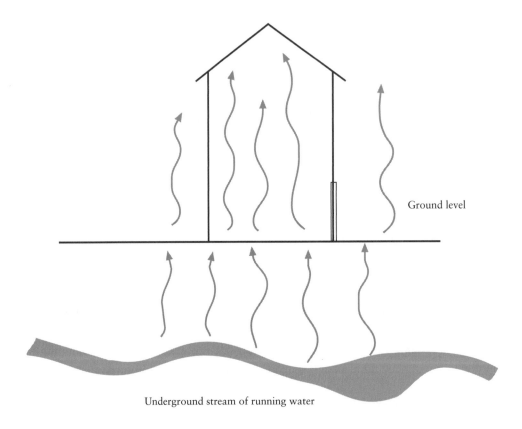

Ground level

Underground stream of running water

Diagram 13.1: Building affected by geopathic stress caused by underground running water.

These geopathic stress rays occur as a result of the friction created by water as it rushes over underground rock surfaces. Sometimes, due to geo-pressure, microwave radiations are also produced that are harmful to health.

European dowsing experts and alternative medical doctors have confirmed that 80 per cent or more of cancer cases are caused by underground geopathic stress. A substantial number of German doctors concur with this research finding. The Dulwich Health Society of the United Kingdom investigated 25,000 cases of patients and confirmed that some form of geopathic stress affected more than 95 per cent of patients with terminal diseases like cancer.

I discovered that when business executives sat over geopathic stress rays, their breathing rate and heartbeat became more rapid. They tired easily, and continually drank coffee to lift their energy. Generally, executives were unable to focus well on their tasks at hand or make sound decisions. Those affected tended to suffer from heart problems and other degenerative diseases and that was why they could not perform. I found that sensitive computer-controlled equipment installed over a geopathic stress area often had faults or malfunctioned if the stress rays were particularly strong.

It is best not to sit or sleep along a geopathic stress line. When unavoidable, geopathic stress rays can be dispersed by using a special plate or "harmonizer" made from natural quartz crystals. It is best to install these devices in the basement, especially in a high-rise building so that it can be free of earth geopathic rays from the ground floor level up to the top floor.

Black streams

The term "black stream" refers to gray or dark, invisible rays that come up from the ground, affecting the lungs and often causing depression. Black streams can be caused by stagnant underground water, cesspools, decayed vegetation, or stagnant water held in old valleys. These rays can cover a width of several yards to over several miles and may contaminate surface water.

Over the last few years severe earthquakes in many parts of the world have caused the release of black streams from underground. A large number of black streams have also formed in Germany, Austria and the USA.

A building, especially for retail business purposes, would be adversely affected if it were situated over an underground black stream. Customers would intuitively feel uncomfortable shopping there. Experienced Feng Shui consultants and geobiology experts use various practical techniques to release or divert the negative energy generated and thus restore the health and vitality of the land, and the people and businesses affected. It is prudent and makes good economic sense to engage the services of an experienced Feng Shui consultant who has a good knowledge of earth energies to check out a construction site. Unnecessary high costs can be avoided, as once a building has been constructed the cost of implementing Feng Shui remedies is considerably higher.

Earth fault lines

Earth fault lines are cracks in the earth's crust, caused by underground earth movements, earthquakes or bomb explosions (see Diagram 13.2). The deeper the cracks, the more dangerous these fault lines are to human and animal health.

Fault line cracks often occur for a long distance, from several yards to several miles. They cause rolling waves of earth energies to surge up, causing severe stress and disturbing work performance.

Earth vortexes

Earth vortexes are spirals of aggressive earth gases or energies moving from under the ground. Often they are caused by certain mineral concentrations, underground caves, or are generated where fault lines cross. Generally, earth vortexes are negative and cause health and work performance problems when a person sits above them.

There are also positive earth vortexes. In ancient times, the European, American Native Indians and the Chinese Taoist masters made use of these vortexes for many good purposes. Very often, big boulders were placed over vortexes that had a positive clockwise spin to harness the earth energies for healing and for ritual purposes (see Diagram 13.5). Ancient, isolated, freestanding stones can still be found in Ireland, the United Kingdom and other parts of Europe.

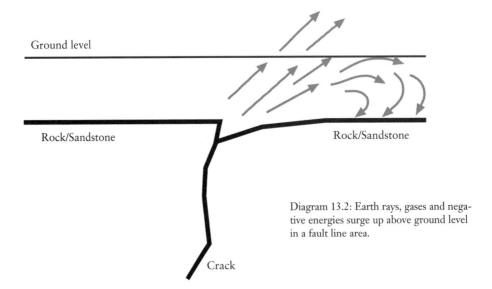

Diagram 13.2: Earth rays, gases and negative energies surge up above ground level in a fault line area.

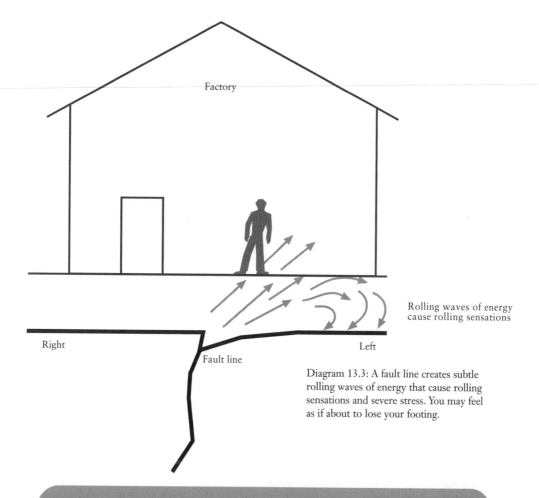

Factory

Rolling waves of energy
cause rolling sensations

Right

Left

Fault line

Diagram 13.3: A fault line creates subtle
rolling waves of energy that cause rolling
sensations and severe stress. You may feel
as if about to lose your footing.

Case study

A fault line cuts along the middle of a factory in Austria. Employees working on
the right side of the building had a feeling that the ground underneath them
was always moving, a sensation caused by the upsurge of earth radiation and
other energies. Many accidents occurred, especially on the right side of the factory. Employees on the right side also had a higher incidence of health problems. The floor of the factory was even cracked along the middle.

Several Feng Shui remedies were carried out and the aggressive upsurge of
earth radiation was dispersed and neutralized. Had the site been carefully
checked out before construction by an experienced Feng Shui consultant, all
the accidents and associated business problems could have been avoided.

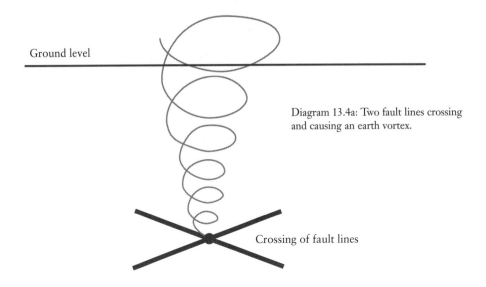

Ground level

Diagram 13.4a: Two fault lines crossing and causing an earth vortex.

Crossing of fault lines

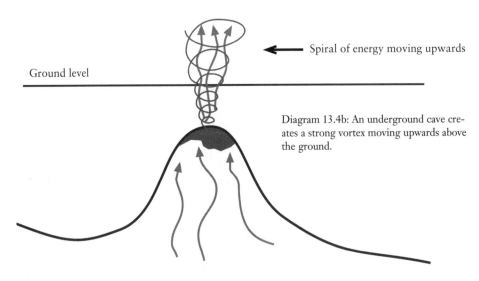

Spiral of energy moving upwards

Ground level

Diagram 13.4b: An underground cave creates a strong vortex moving upwards above the ground.

Underground cave

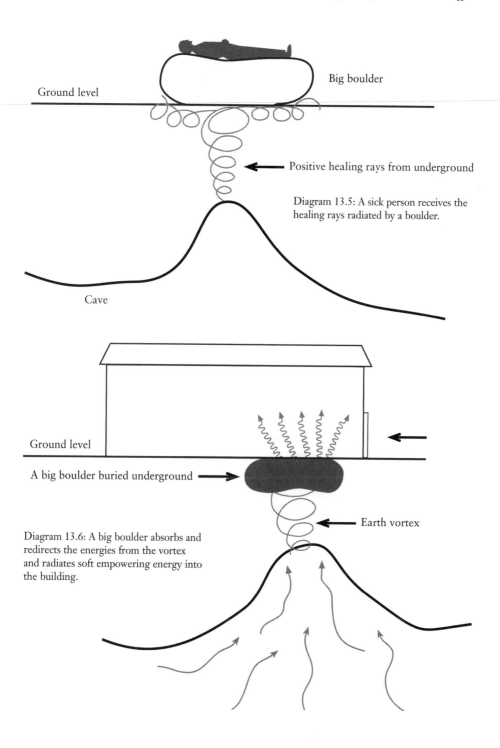

Ground level

Big boulder

Positive healing rays from underground

Diagram 13.5: A sick person receives the healing rays radiated by a boulder.

Cave

Ground level

A big boulder buried underground

Earth vortex

Diagram 13.6: A big boulder absorbs and redirects the energies from the vortex and radiates soft empowering energy into the building.

Business premises can harness a positive earth vortex to improve the vitality of the workers and attract customers. I found that if a business had a powerful positive vortex in the foyer area, it attracted exceptionally large numbers of customers. The radiated soft healing energies attract cosmic life force energy and oxygen and thereby become a catalyst to attract more customers (see Diagram 13.6). An experienced Feng Shui consultant with a sound knowledge of geobiology would be able to identify positive earth vortexes and design empowered business premises.

Computer radiation and electrosmog

With the fast-changing conditions in the workplace of the twenty-first century, there comes a need for more speed and a higher level of performance, which causes much additional stress. This is already a way of life for many people. The wide range of electronic equipment, although necessary for enhancing speed and efficiency in the workplace, radiates plenty of electric, magnetic and electromagnetic fields that generate much electrosmog and thus more stress. Scientific evidence is now available to confirm heavy electrosmog weakens the immune system.

In the modern office, computers and other electronic equipment are essential for its efficient operation. Manufacturers usually aim to reduce the production cost and shorten the marketing cycle of their products, and in their expediency they do not check the harmful effects of their equipment on the people who have to operate it.

Intensive research in Canada and the UK has confirmed that there is a higher incidence of birth defects in babies whose mothers operated computers during their pregnancy. The known birth defects include damage of organs such as the heart and an under-functioning of the immune system. Kinesiologists using their specialized techniques, and doctors in Germany and the UK using bio-feedback machines, discovered that when people sit in front of a modern computer regularly they show a disturbance of the body's electrical circuit and a weakening of the immune system.

The radiation produced by a computer can be measured up to six feet (two metres) away in any direction, even if a partition is placed in between. A partition does not give safe protection from the electromagnetic radiation or the radio and microwave rays produced by some computers. However, partial protection can be given by placing rounded natural quartz crystals, three times the size of an adult thumb, in front of and at the back of a computer, to disperse the radiations coming from the computer.

Electrosmog in modern offices is also bad for health. When breathed in it causes the lung cells to swell resulting in a lowered oxygen intake. This reaction may cause allergies. To counter this problem, windows should be opened often to flush out the electrosmog. An efficient ventilation system is an essential facility in an office using many computers and other electronic equipment.

Modern healthy offices can be specifically designed to avoid heavy electrosmog at no additional cost. Understandably, only specialized architects with a knowledge of building biology can offer this type of design, as most university schools of architecture do not have such technology and methods in their curriculum.

Toxins in offices

First, I would like to mention some factors about toxins and electrical radiation:

> *In the construction of modern office buildings and stores, a vast range of materials is used. Synthetic materials may produce toxic gases. In the field of building biology, hundreds of toxins have been identified — for example, formaldehyde, benzene, chloroform, xylene, toluene, acetone, ammonia, and trichloroethylene.*

> *Swiss and Austrian studies have confirmed that modern concrete buildings reinforced by steel bars are generating negative radiations that can be measured up to twelve inches (thirty centimetres) from internal walls.*

> *Another problem is the toxic air in buildings. For better soundproofing and energy conservation, modern buildings are completely sealed off from the fresh air circulating outside. The air inside buildings tends to be dry and some offices use a humidifier. Although the moisture spread by the humidifier is affected by magnetic fields, it can at least neutralize some of the electrosmog and slightly help to improve the quality of air.*

> *Modern offices built during the last twenty years have many electrical sockets and operate a lot of modern high-tech equipment like computers, copiers and fax machines, generating strong electrical and magnetic fields causing harmful electrosmog.*

> *American and Russian scientists discovered that when humans are in a confined space they release more than 150 volatile substances apart from carbon dioxide. The amount of toxic gases and toxins released by a person is based on the condition of their health and the food they consume. A person can therefore contribute to the toxicity that makes their colleagues sick.*

Common health problems

Our ancestors a hundred years ago would have died a premature death working in these highly air-polluted modern offices. The most common health problems recorded in modern polluted offices are allergies, eye, nose and throat irritations, headache, sinus and respiratory congestion, tinnitus (ear ringing), asthma and general fatigue. These health problems have cost businesses billions annually in work productivity losses.

Sick buildings

Although air conditioning has solved some of the indoor air circulation problems, an air-conditioning system itself is a health hazard. It is impossible to clean all the ducting and filters regularly. When I interviewed air-conditioning maintenance companies, I was surprised to hear that air-conditioning filters were cleaned either once in six months or annually. Bacteria and fungi are often found growing in poorly ventilated buildings and there is a higher incidence of sickness among the office workers.

I remember in the 1970s working in a modern office building in Singapore's busy Orchard Road. About one third of the office staff, including myself, had to see our company's doctor at least once a month for lung and allergy problems. This 1960s building in present-day terms would be called a "sick" building. A building affected by a "black stream" or earth fault-lines tends to have a higher level of fungi and bacteria and also belongs to the "sick building" group.

What you can do about indoor air pollution

We lose 70 to 80 per cent of natural fresh air when we erect a building and shut doors and windows. Our best way to stay healthy indoors is to go back to nature for answers. Nature shows us the two best solutions: running water and indoor plants. Healthy growing plants, both indoors and outdoors, provide the best support.

In fact humans developed from a similar source as plants. The DNA structure of our cells is in many instances similar to that of plants (see Diagram 2.10 in chapter 2). This symbol of life, with three sets of figure eights clustered together, is found both in plants and in human cells. Plants are in many ways more sensitive and responsive to environmental conditions than we are. We can therefore communicate mentally or verbally with plants. Plants can sense whether we are friendly or aggressive and react accordingly.

Plants in offices and stores

Plants provide the second most important Feng Shui remedy after water. The green color has a relaxing effect and looking at flowering plants enhances our well-being. Correctly placed, big bushy plants may even reduce noise. All offices should have at least one plant three feet (one metre) in height to keep the air in an office clean and healthy. If there are many computers and electrical devices in the office, at least two bushy plants should be put up for filtering the air. Sick plants should be removed immediately as they may present a health hazard. If you do not have a "green thumb" you can rent plants and have them exchanged every two weeks.

The rooting medium of a plant should preferably be earth so that the bacteria in the earth can break down the toxins, microbes and pollutants absorbed by the plants. Solid, burnt-clay granules are not suitable for this purpose. It is advisable to replace some of the soil each year, to remove toxins and maintain the health and efficiency of the plants. If it is very dark, additional plant lights should be used.

What plants for what toxins?

The US National Aeronautics and Space Administration (NASA) has conducted extensive research on toxin absorption by indoor plants. Different types of plants were used in the space shuttles to keep astronauts healthy during space travel. The plants listed in Table 13 are most efficient in removing common toxins and harmful gases from the air.

Table 13: Plants for Removing Indoor Toxins	
Formaldehyde	Gerbera, daisy, Janet Craig, bamboo palm, dwarf date palm, rubber plant, English ivy, weeping fig, peace lily, dragon tree.
Xylene and Toluene	Dwarf date palm, dragon tree, peace lily
Radiations	Mother-in-law plant (snake plant), aloe vera, kalanchoe.

Modern offices should reserve a small "garden area" with many plants and copious running water to cleanse and reactivate the air twenty-four hours a day. Indoor fountains and gardens contribute to a much better quality of air and attract more cosmic Qi. Of course, these remedies need to be correctly placed according to Feng Shui practice and in harmony with the occupants to receive the maximum benefit.

According to the Five Elements Principle in Feng Shui, a person should not have plants inside an enclosed office within six feet (two metres) of his or her physical body if the birth year element is Earth or Metal. Plants belong to the Wood element and drain an Earth person's energy (Wood breaks up Earth), and a person with a Metal element would be in constant conflict with the plants (Metal cuts Wood). This conflict would reduce the positive effect of the plants.

Communicate with your plants

It is much easier to communicate with plants than with animals. Before we cut plants or raw vegetables we should communicate with them to reduce the toxicity. One of my students in Austria was very friendly and nurturing to her plants. When she went on vacation for two months, she told her plants to look after themselves and obtain food from outside the apartment. From a long distance she mentally communicated daily to all her plants in her apartment. On her return she found that not only were the plants robust and healthy, many had flowers in full bloom. She found the earth that held the plants was completely dry and normal plants would have dehydrated and died. Indeed, the plants obtain food nutrients and water from the air. Plants can be encouraged to purify your office air if you communicate with them and treat them with love.

Plants to avoid

Not all plants are suitable for offices. The Yucca palm is a desert plant and has a strong survival instinct. This plant "attacks" office visitors and customers with its sharp-pointed leaves. This is an easy plant to grow, but it cannot be placed in an office where you need to see customers. I know of three businesses in Zurich, Innsbruck and Hong Kong that have gone bankrupt because each office placed a large Yucca plant in front of the office doorway and in the foyer without realizing that the plants were directing harmful energies to the customers as they came in.

The familiar *Ficus benjamina* is an excellent plant with plenty of leaves to cleanse the air, but it must not be placed near a heater or next to the windows during summer. When too hot, this plant emits toxic fumes that may cause asthma, lung problems or allergies.

Fern plants with fine hair on the back of the leaves are not suitable for offices that are air-conditioned. The fine hair of these plants can cause allergy and asthma attacks, and the air conditioning system will blow the allergens around the office.

Cacti and any plants with long, sharp leaves are aggressive plants that are not suitable for placement in business premises.

Chapter 14
Feng Shui and the Structure of Organizations

Humans, like all living creatures, feel safer when living in groups or in communities. Over a long period of time a relatively rigid hierarchical structure was predominant. However, the new millennium creates new challenges for the individual as well as the group. This is the time to create new, flexible and more powerful organizational structures.

The pyramid structure
It is a fact that 80 per cent of any group of people, be they in a family, a village, a religious community or any other type of group, are not always capable of making rational decisions on their own. Many people are used to letting others make the major decisions for them. That is why, throughout history, we have observed large numbers of people who were more or less willing to be enslaved by working long hours with little pay or no reward. Many were even prepared to give up their lives in order to protect their enslavement. Up until the 1950s, the tribal and government structure was in the form of a pyramid. Business organizations were structured and managed along similar lines.

The pyramid structure was usually controlled autocratically by one person — by a king, a boss, or a tribal leader, with a few senior assistants to help govern and control. Authority was rigid and often brutally enforced to ensure obedience and subservience. The straight lines down the sides of the pyramid represent this type of authority.

A steep pyramid structure can only work when more than 90 per cent of a population or workforce is not well educated or is lacking in knowledge. This type of structure is not a beneficial structure according to nature's harmonic flow, and causes bad energy and inefficiency from the restricted "bottleneck" at the top.

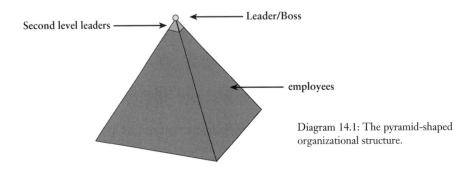

Diagram 14.1: The pyramid-shaped organizational structure.

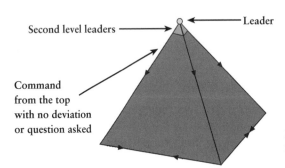

Diagram 14.2: Straight lines indicating rigid authority.

Pyramid business organization

In a pyramid business organization there was no major incentive to follow orders of the chief or boss except for survival and supporting the family. There is a complete lack of innovation and creativity in these communities. Before the 1960s most business organizations were run with very rigid structures. In the 1960s and 1970s, when more countries became independent with elected governments, the rigid autocratic human pyramid changed slightly because there were more elected leaders to help run and govern countries and communities. With more efficient delegation, organizations became bigger and more people were employed. The pyramid became less steep and had a wider base due to the organizational structure.

LEADERSHIP

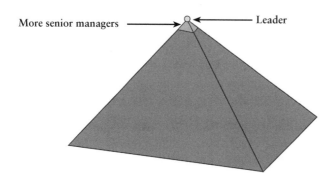

Diagram 14.3: In the 1960s and 1970s, the base of pyramid organizational structure became broader, with more senior staff through delegation and with more staff employed.

In the 1980s and 1990s, with more educated citizens, the organizational structure in business and communities also substantially changed. More groups in communities and businesses became involved in the running of the organizations. This structure allowed for more independent thinking, innovation and creativity that then resulted in a wide range of new innovative products flooding the markets. The organizational structure changed its form to an inverted pendulum.

This inverted, pendulum-shaped human organization in business is still not the best shape to suit the twenty-first century. The new century is a communication age with more interactions at all levels of an organization. The inverted-pendulum organization is still rigid with many straight lines causing inflexibility. Straight lines in human organizations still contain lots of autocratic energy — a sign of inner conflict and fear amongst employees. This situation in offices creates bad vibrations and bad Feng Shui that weakens the overall performance of a business. One unhappy employee can adversely affect the performance of other employees with whom there is conflict. For future success, business organizations will need to adopt a pear-shaped structure or Feng Shui organizational structure (see Diagram 14.5).

Diagram 14.4: An inverted pendulum shape organizational structure. This structure allows for wider participation and encourages some entrepreneurial activity. The 1980s and 1990s are considered to be the age of the pendulum organization.

Feng Shui organizational structure

A pear-shaped organizational structure is smooth, gradually getting larger near the base and smaller at the top. There is a core stem in the middle to allow feedback and interaction with top management.

The pear-shaped organization has more active leaders — for example, more major shareholders and more executive directors to make major decisions, after receiving continual feedback from the whole organization through the core stem. Many section leaders are running lean, very active teams. They work independently with minimum interference from the top levels. There is a lot of interaction and feedback between sections, as seen from the horizontal arrows merging with the vertical arrows as they move up from the base into the middle, and then up the core stem. Routine and mundane jobs and services like transport, packaging and mailing deliveries, for example, are contracted out for better efficiency (outsourcing).

A pear-shaped business organization is considered the best to reflect the new awakening awareness of the Aquarian Age in the new millennium. It is an age of fast communication. Any business with a pear-shaped organization is flowing with nature and time, creating a powerful, cohesive, caring and happy organization in which to work. Production time for new products is also considerably reduced. People working in such organizations are creative and empowered to succeed.

Diagram 14.5: The pear-shaped organizational structure is needed for the economy of the 21st century.

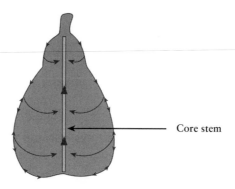

Core stem

This type of organization tends to make fewer mistakes and performs better than its competitors in similar fields. The pear shape is called the *Feng Shui organization*. There is a mix of natural, harmonic energy and happy, communicative people. They create a highly vitalized and well-informed organization and workplace that is conducive to peace and harmony while enhancing success and peak performance.

A Feng Shui organizational structure makes an organization more humane and caring, allowing lots of opportunities for entrepreneurs and creative people — a recipe for competitiveness and success.

The direction for business in the new millennium

Most large business organizations generally lack creativity and are unable to produce innovative products quickly and competitively. Many large conglomerates and multi-national groups are seeking to gain an advantage with takeovers. When they merge with companies that produce the same products, they can then pool their resources and reduce their costs in management and research. But they are trying to re-create the pyramid structure that was repressive and blocked independent thinking, innovation and entrepreneurial participation. Unless large companies change their organizational structures from the large, rigid, pyramid structure to multiples of small Feng Shui organizations that operate independently, they have little chance of success after the year 2008. The year 2008 is the time when the Aquarian Age officially starts, and will be an age of speed and rapid innovation. The twenty-first century is a computer age with easy, high-speed access to information and knowledge. Only small groups of dedicated Feng Shui organizations will be able to move at the necessary speed to innovate — and win.

CHAPTER 15
Your Quest for Success and Happiness

Everyone wants to earn a good income to support his or her family and have a good life. Some people are able to earn high incomes easily, while others have to struggle for a living. The Chinese and Indians believe that our present experience is the result of past actions, including those from previous lives — they call it *karma*.

The concept of karma is based on both the cause and effect of our mental and emotional reactions to people, and our personal physical actions. Many people think that it is unlikely one is reborn or has karmic connections, or else completely reject the idea. For a long time the Christian church has also strictly rejected the concept of reincarnation. Yet, in the texts of early Christianity there are indications that human reincarnation exists. It is interesting to note that Pope John Paul II recently made a statement confirming that there is a possible past life. Many readers may be skeptical of the contents of this chapter, but just read on and then make your own decision.

Factors that determine success
According to a Westerner's view, people are apt to be more successful if they have the following features or qualities:

> *Pleasant personality and high vitality*

> *Good sales techniques and the ability to promote oneself*

> *Good connections*

> *Luck*
> *The ability to make good decisions with intuitive guidance*
> *Good professional knowledge*
> *Academic qualifications*

Why do people who grew up in the same neighborhood and went to the same schools later achieve vastly different levels of success in life? The Chinese, since the time of Confucius, have subscribed to many of these same beliefs as to why one person is substantially different from another. From my own experience, working with many nationalities and observing their progress through life, I have over the last thirty years developed a slightly different perspective on the success factors of a person:

> *Your family, your birth horoscope and your name*
> *A pleasant personality and high vitality*
> *Your spiritual sensitivity and your intuitive ability*
> *Your right profession — your life calling*
> *Good professional knowledge*
> *Good connections*
> *Feng Shui to enhance vitality and luck*
> *Suitable professional qualifications*
> *Academic qualifications*

These nine factors can be summarized into what the Chinese call *Heaven-Earth-Human* factors. When all of these three factors are in harmony, then it is only natural to expect a person to be more successful than others.

Heaven represents your birth (your past karma), influenced by the cosmos and planets. *Earth* is the environment and landscape in which you live, and is connected with Feng Shui. *Human* is how you acquire living knowledge and how you interact and respond to other people and conditions.

Creativity is the key to wealth

Feng Shui therefore features very prominently in all three *Heaven-Earth-Human* factors. Feng Shui can help a person find suitable land and powerful energy places to work and live, and empower them with vitality and energy to perform at their peak.

We are all living in an interdependent world. The better the services and products you can create, and the more people who are helped as a result, the more you are rewarded.

Improve prosperity consciousness

To be successful, a person has to awaken their prosperity consciousness to be more generous and willing to share. There is no limit to the size of the wealth cake and the number of pieces. The more creative a person is, the larger their wealth cake becomes. There does not need to be any fear of not having enough. History has proven that fear of not having enough has been the most frequent cause of wars, fighting and destruction in all kinds of cultures.

To have good prosperity and wealth, a person should never think of the money reward for whatever they want to do. Research and history has overwhelmingly shown that successful projects and business results come about through an overwhelming commitment by a person or a group of people to implement an idea that provides a superior service to their community or society in general. In almost all cases of those who are very successful, monetary reward was not the main focus. An overwhelming focus on the monetary gain most often results in the failure of projects. I have personally evaluated more than twenty highly profitable projects that failed when money and profits were the prime focus.

A German success story

A German doctor observed the problems in serving quick lunches that were often unhealthy junk food. He also recognized the problems faced by the food caterers in serving quick meals. He wanted to find a way to mass-produce healthy meals in factories to then sell to food caterers. He found the solution after several years and became a multimillionaire without realizing his worth or the net worth of his company. He was greatly surprised when an offer was made to buy his company for several hundred million German marks. He sold his business, retired and reinvested his money in real estate.

How is it that many people work very hard and smart, but never become wealthy enough to retire? The difference lies in a person's creativity!

Success, wealth and spirituality

I have found that many people with low incomes have a feeling of guilt towards money, and believe that wealth is dirty and unspiritual. This is not correct. In fact the most spiritual people are those with the high spiritual sensitivity that gives them the benefit of an intuitive knowing. That then guides right thinking and sound decisions to make these people the most successful people in the world. They run multi-billion-dollar companies and are also the heads of governments. By the way, religious institutions like the Roman Catholic Church are among the richest institutions in the world.

Wealth created by lawful and skilful means exemplifies good deeds. Wealth can create industries, businesses and jobs. Wealth creates abundance in the supply of food and homes and satisfies all the basic necessities of life. With sufficiency there is less fear of somebody taking away your share. In circumstances of abundance, people tend to live a happier life with less conflict and destruction.

Factors in creating prosperity and wealth

The following is a list of some important guidelines successful people apply that can contribute to your prosperity and increased wealth:

> *Your ability to create a special or unique service, or goods to supply a special need.*

> *You must spend more to create more to share, to allow a free flow of wealth to induce or attract more.*

> *Have a strong belief that you are helping your fellow men and women with your skills, service or products.*

> *Know when the timing is right to capitalize.*

> *Your prosperity is the perception of the worth of your service. The same meal, article or service may be sold at different values to different groups.*

> *Wealth creation is the result of using the special skills one has to multiply success.*

> *Wealth can also be created through other people multiplying your skills or products (e.g., licensing, franchising).*

> *Be generous to your staff and have good virtue.*

> *Have the courage and commitment to try and be prepared to fail if need be.*

An Australian success story

An Australian office consultant, Mr. B, worked very hard. He usually worked fifty hours a week and refused to employ additional senior staff to help him. He always had problems paying his bills. His intuitive wife could sense that many things were not right for her husband. She asked for a Feng Shui consultation of her husband's office and a personal consultation to help her husband overcome his workaholic attitude and money problems.

I told him and his wife that some Feng Shui remedies could improve his business, but he felt constrained by a shortage of staff. I recommended a past life therapy to discover why he had such a fear of employing people. Like most businessmen, he did not believe in past lives and was skeptical, but agreed to give past life therapy a try.

During the therapy, he went back two hundred years to peasant Russia. He was a serf who rented land from a noble family in order to plant food. His family rented a large acreage and was a very successful farming family. Because he was not a nobleman, the noble family and officials of the time told him that wealth was not good for him. He was then asked to give some land back to the noble family to lease to more people so that the landlords could receive higher rents. Once he had returned a lot of the land, he was then asked to employ more people to work his rented land. Eventually the landlords and the people he employed forced him to leave his land.

The insight he gained from this past life helped him understand the specific relationship to his present life. He held a subconscious belief that wanting to be rich got him into trouble. He therefore subconsciously concluded that to avoid trouble it was better to have less money and not employ others. This is exactly what he was doing in his own business, like two hundred years ago, by refusing to employ additional senior staff whom he saw as a threat to his business.

As a result of the past life experience Mr. B became aware of his problems and fear and was able to change his behavior. He is now a very successful businessman employing ten times more staff and working fewer hours every day.

An American success story

In another case, an experienced and highly qualified American engineer, Mr. A, was very skilful in commencing road and engineering projects. However, during the last phase of any project he undertook, his superior observed with great frustration that he was unable to complete a project on time. As a result, he was bypassed for several promotions and substantial salary increases.

His boss asked him to consult me. I took Mr. A back to a past life, five hundred years ago when he was an English engineer, supervising the construction of an arched bridge in North London. On its completion the bridge collapsed and many people died as a result. He was not totally to blame because some flooding several weeks before had weakened the foundation. However, this past life memory had left a lasting impression to the effect that he believed if he completed a project a disaster would occur. This hidden fear was the reason he delayed completing his assigned projects in this life.

Once Mr. A was consciously aware that this past bad experience was the cause of his present work problems, he went on to perform well in his job. He received several promotions before he retired comfortably.

My own story

I can relate my own experience with past life therapy, which I came upon as a last resort. When I was young I was exceptionally fearful of heights. My job required me to travel extensively throughout South-East Asia, yet the mere mention of traveling caused me anguish and fear. I lost many good job opportunities because they would have required me to travel regularly by plane.

I went through more than one hundred hours of psychotherapy in several different countries, and yet this therapy did not solve my problem. I was told to learn to fly, which I did, and received my pilot's license. My fear of heights persisted. A famous American woman, Denise Linn, author of many books on dreams and past lives, took me back to a past life about two hundred and fifty years ago when I fell into the Grand Canyon and died. This therapy solved my fear of heights forever.

These stories highlight the fact that when we are faced with an obstacle that blocks us from being able to achieve our desired goal and objective, it is important to seek help immediately. Very often we find solutions in the most unlikely places.

Be open and adventurous enough to give even something unusual like past life therapy a try. In many parts of the world, past life therapy is an accepted form of treatment of emotional and behavioral problems.

Feng Shui and success

I have worked with billionaires, multimillionaires, and chief executives of large multinational companies in many countries. These successful people are always well focused and disciplined. They quickly solve problems that are affecting them. When they have a personal problem, they recognize it and quickly seek therapy or additional study and training to overcome their shortcomings. Many of them have exceptional stamina and courage to stand up and try again and again after they have failed, as if nothing serious has happened.

Entrepreneurs and senior executives of business enterprises with strong personalities and characters tend to be able to overcome, or seek help to overcome, any inherent weakness that might prevent them achieving their desired goals. Due to the high speed of business dealings and the quickly changing business environment, successful entrepreneurs and chief executives of many large corporations are seeking solutions outside of mainstream knowledge sources. Many smart business leaders have personal coaches and gurus to help them solve problems.

Traditional universities and colleges, burdened by bureaucracy and politics, are unable to respond to present business conditions and lifestyle requirements. Many "old culture" practices, like Business Feng Shui (which has been practiced by the Chinese for more than three thousand years), are regarded as esoteric and unacceptable by the universities. Yet you have read the contents of this book and much of it is part of daily business practice around the world.

Business Feng Shui practice is the guarded secret of successful entrepreneurs and top business executives in Asia. This practice will soon become a mainstream practice in the West.

APPENDIX

Eight Trigrams East–West Building System: Point System

To help readers select the most auspicious areas in a room, points are allocated for each area of a building or room. The most auspicious area will have the highest plus score (also refer to end of chapter 9).

Building Trigram

Auspicious areas

AA	A1	A2	A3
+80	+70	+60	+55

Inauspicious areas

D4	D3	D2	D1
–90	–85	–70	–60

Personal Trigram Locations

Auspicious Directions/Locations

AA	A1	A2	A3
+50	+40	+30	+20

Inauspicious Directions/Locations

D4	D3	D2	D1
–60	–50	–40	–30

Building Trigram ratings score higher points than individual Personal Life Trigram ratings, because a room covers a larger area than a human body and the room energy exerts a stronger influence on the occupants than vice versa.

Example: If a person occupies an A1 area in an office you add +70. If the area a person occupies is in a D4 area, then the person deducts –90 from the point score.

If an office has an A1 rating with +70 (also refer to Diagrams 9.7 and 9.8) and the Personal Trigram rating is A3 with +20, then the total for this office is +90 (+70+20=90). This room is therefore auspicious.

If an office that a person occupies has an A1 (+70) rating (see Diagrams 10.7 and 10.8), and it happens that his/her Personal Life Trigram rating has an A3 rating (+20), then the score for this office is +90 (+70 + 20 = +90). This is therefore an auspicious room for him/her to occupy.

Comparing the element of the Room Trigram and the element of the Personal Life Trigram:

Supporting (productive cycle): +35
Example: Water (room)   Wood (personal)

Neutral (same element): +20
Example: Wood (room)   Wood (personal)

Draining (Mother-child cycle): –35
Example: Fire (room)   Wood (personal)

Conflict (element of person destroys room element): –35
Example: Wood (room)   Metal (personal)

Conflict (element of room destroys element of person): –45
Example: Metal (room)   Wood (personal)

About the Author

In the 1960s Jes T. Y. Lim became a trained corporate consultant in Great Britain and Malaysia. He was a general manager and chief executive in subsidiary branches of multinational companies such as Sime Darby, Inchcape and Fletcher Challenge Group in Australasia. He gained his experience mainly in the areas of turnaround and corporate recovery, applying Business Feng Shui in every project.

Dr. Lim has studied Feng Shui, geomancy, geobiology and natural medicine with teachers in China, Hong Kong, Singapore, Malaysia, Sri Lanka and Australia. He was a member of the British Institute of Management, fellow of the Chartered Institute of Marketing, UK, and a member of the Organisation and Methods Institute, UK. Dr. Lim has a diploma in psychology and hypnotherapy (New Zealand) and a degree in natural medicine (Australia), as well as a Master's Degree in International Business Administration (USA). Dr. Lim is also a doctor of acupuncture (Sri Lanka and China).

Dr. Lim is the founder, president and dean of the Qi-Mag International Feng Shui & Geobiology Institute, which is offering courses up to the master's degree in 15 countries worldwide.

The Courses

Courses offered by the Qi-Mag Feng Shui & Geobiology Institute are held in Australia, China, Hong Kong, Singapore, India, USA, Germany, Austria, Switzerland and other EU countries.

Qi-Mag Feng Shui I
Practical "First Aid Feng Shui" for house and apartment. Common Feng Shui problems and remedies that can be applied immediately.

Qi-Mag Feng Shui II
Selecting auspicious areas in rooms and buildings that are harmonious with an individual. Selection of auspicious Trigram areas for sleeping and working to enhance vitality, success and abundance. Five Elements principle, yin and yang harmony, Eight Trigrams and Feng Shui astrological system.

Qi-Mag Business Feng Shui
First comprehensive and practical Business Feng Shui course for the workplace and commercial buildings to enhance success. Design of positive logos and symbols for business. Study of ancient, subtle techniques to empower peak performance.

Qi-Mag Feng Shui Consultant Course I & II
Intensive, including the following topics: Landscape Feng Shui, auspicious designs for house and flat, Eight Trigrams East–West System using the Lo'pan, astrological aspects and interpretations — for example, the Lo'Shu system of flying stars.

Participants will receive the International Feng Shui Consultant Diploma (FSC) for worldwide practice after attending Feng Shui Consultant I & II.

Qi-Mag Feng Shui Consultant Course III
Water Dragon and Landscape Feng Shui: types of water, types of mountains and their effects on humans, towns and cities. Application and design of fountains, waterfalls and other Feng Shui remedies using water to increase business success and attract customers.

Feng Shui Architecture & Design I–IV
Level I – Design of healthy residences with high energy for vital living.
Level II – Design for harmonious and successful business buildings as well as interior design.

Participants receive the international diploma Feng Shui Architecture & Consultant for Home and Commercial Buildings (FSARCH) after attending courses I & II.

Advanced Courses – Levels III & IV

Environmental and geomancy design for landscape, town planning and traffic, including techniques to enhance the success and prosperity of towns and cities.

Master Courses – Advanced Feng Shui Master Techniques, Qi-Mag Geomancy and Geobiology I & II

Study of earth and environmental energies and everyday application of positive energies. Health aspects and building design; designing an eco-friendly environment; increasing plant yields without artificial fertilizers.

N.B.: Advanced courses can only be attended by those with a Diploma in FSARCH or FSC. On completion of Consultant I–VIII and practical work, participants will receive an International Degree in Feng Shui and Geobiology. All Consultant, Advanced Architecture, and Master Courses are taught by Prof. Dr. Lim. All courses are held in English and Chinese and can be translated into German or other local languages.

For more information on courses presented in North America, please visit the web site www.fengshuicanada.net.

Look for these other great books at your favorite bookstore:

Hot Lemon & Honey
Reflections for success in times of stress and change
Catherine DeVrye

Internationally known motivational speaker Catherine DeVrye shows how to make your personal and professional life more meaningful and how to regain control in these hectic times. Using catchy phrases and memorable real-life examples, DeVrye encourages readers to revitalize their thinking, leading to less stress and a return to the joyous life. ISBN 1-894622-25-1

The Vegetarian Traveler
A guide to eating green in 197 countries
Bryan Geon

Vegetarians and people who wish to avoid eating meat for health reasons when traveling often encounter linguistic and cultural barriers while on the road. *The Vegetarian Traveler* is the first guide to the words and phrases needed to order vegetarian foods in over 200 countries and territories. World traveler and long-time vegetarian Bryan Geon also gives informative and witty insights into what to expect when attempting to order meatless meals around the world. ISBN 1-894020-85-5

How to Survive Without a Salary
Learning how to live the Conserver Lifestyle
Charles Long

Too many of us trade our happiness and well-being for the reliability of a steady paycheck. Is there any way out of this dilemma? Charles Long offers one possibility — the Conserver Lifestyle. Long shows you how to reduce your cash needs to a level you can easily meet with casual income so that you can live the life you've always dreamed of. This is not a dreary tome about budgeting, however — Long draws on his own family's decades of experience livng without a salary for amusing anecdotes that confirm conserving as a joyful, liberating way to live. ISBN 1-894622-37-5

Please visit our website, www.warwickgp.com, for more information about our books.